THE AP EUROPEAN HISTORY STUDY GUIDE 2024

Everything You Need to Know to Ace SAQ, DBQ & LEQ, Get an A in Your Class and Score a 5 on The APEH Exam Day

By
The Hartley Publishing

COPYRIGHT AND DISCLAIMER

By using this study guide, you agree to the terms and conditions of this Copyright and Disclaimer statement.

TABLE OF CONTENTS

INTRODUCTION

Delving into the intricate web of Europe's history, from the era of the Renaissance till today, can be a daunting task even for the most devoted learners. We understand the complex and emotional hurdles you might encounter as you decipher the intricate details of the AP European History examination, an assessment that necessitates a deep understanding of historic incidents, themes, and concepts, and advanced levels of critical thinking and analytical skills. However, with the proper preparation, empathetic study strategies, and unwavering determination, you can conquer this exam and achieve your academic goals.

This guide is your caring and understanding partner in your quest to triumph over the AP Euro exam. This comprehensive guide has been carefully crafted to provide you with tailored strategies for test-taking, in-depth study guides for each historical period, thorough review materials, and an abundance of valuable resources. Our committed crew of seasoned educators, historians, and test preparation specialists have invested their broad knowledge and comprehension in crafting this study guide. Leveraging their long-standing expertise in authorship, publication, and education, our objective is to amplify your exam readiness by arming you with the fundamental knowledge, abilities, and support crucial for your triumph.

By embracing this study guide, you will experience a structured study plan that accommodates your unique needs, efficient strategies that respect your valuable time, and comprehensive explanations of question types and formats delivered with empathy. Our carefully crafted practice questions, prompts, and sample essays have been developed with the recognition that each student learns differently and may face various emotional challenges, and they are designed to mirror the rigor and expectations of the AP Euro exam. We have incorporated key terms, a timeline of momentous events, and a curated selection of primary source documents to help you forge a deeper connection with the historical context and enhance your ability to analyze primary and secondary sources.

We acknowledge students' emotional obstacles and pressures as they prepare for the AP European History exam. Rest assured that the efficacy of this study guide is supported by the accomplishments of our previous students, who have employed our empathetic methods to achieve top scores on the AP Euro exam and excel in their coursework. Under our compassionate guidance, you, too, can reach these heights of success, surpass your own expectations, and unlock your true academic potential.

Are you prepared to embrace your exam preparation, confront the challenge head-on, and weave your own distinctive narrative with the help of this guide? Allow us to accompany you on this enthralling and enlightening journey through the annals of European history, extending understanding, encouragement, and empathy at every step. Together, we can aid you in navigating the complexities of your academic pursuits and surmounting any challenges that may arise, fostering an environment of growth, resilience, and achievement.

EXAM FORMAT AND STRUCTURE

The AP European History Exam is a comprehensive assessment that evaluates students' grasp and comprehension of European history concepts, events, and analytical skills. The exam spans a duration of 3 hours and 15 minutes, and it comprises two primary sections, each subdivided into two components: Section I - Multiple Choice and Short Answer, and Section II - Document-Based and Long Essay questions.

Section I (Multiple Choice and Short Answer)

Part A: Multiple Choice

The Multiple Choice segment of the AP European History Exam comprises 55 questions designed to assess your familiarity and comprehension of critical events, themes, and concepts that cover European history.

Multiple choice questions in the AP European History Exam typically appear in sets of 2 to 5. These questions are often based on a stimulus, which can include primary and secondary sources, images, graphs, or maps. The stimulus material serves as the foundation for the questions, requiring you to analyze and interpret the information presented in the source. The content covered in the multiple choice section spans the entire scope of European history. You will come across queries encompassing varied epochs, from the Renaissance to the present era. Subjects might incorporate political, economic, social, cultural, and intellectual progress and their influence on Europe and the global stage.

Questions might also probe into significant events like wars, revolutions, and diplomatic negotiations, and the role of influential historical personas who steered the course of European history. Additionally, you might need to scrutinize the reasons and outcomes of specific historical phenomena or follow the progression of particular ideas, institutions, or movements over time.

Analytical Skills Assessed

The multiple-choice section assesses a range of analytical skills crucial for success in studying history.

Some examples of these skills are:

a) Historical Thinking Skills

The questions may test your ability to analyze cause-and-effect relationships, understand continuity and change over time, compare and contrast historical developments, and identify patterns and themes across different time periods.

b) Interpretation of Historical Sources

Some questions may require you to interpret and analyze historical texts, such as speeches, letters, or government documents, and evaluate their relevance, credibility, and significance in the context of the question being asked.

c) Analysis of Visual and Quantitative Sources

You may also encounter questions that involve the analysis of visual sources, such as maps, paintings, or photographs, as well as quantitative sources, like graphs, charts, or tables. These questions test your ability to extract relevant information, draw conclusions, and relate the sources to broader historical themes and contexts.

d) Historiographical Understanding

The multiple choice questions may assess your familiarity with different historians' interpretations of events or historical concepts. During the exam, you might be required to analyze and differentiate diverse perspectives, appraise the advantages and disadvantages of contrasting viewpoints, or evaluate the progression of historical interpretations throughout time.

Scoring for Section I – Part A: Multiple Choice

The Multiple Choice section of the AP European History Exam plays a significant role in determining your final score, as it constitutes 40% of the total exam score.

To understand how your performance in this section impacts your overall score and how to calculate it, let's explore the scoring process and its various components:

1. Raw Score Calculation

Determining your raw score is the first step in calculating your Section I - Part A score. The raw score stands for the cumulative count of correctly answered questions. Each multiple-choice query carries an identical value, and there are no deductions for wrong answers. Thus, your raw score equates to the total number of correctly responded questions out of the 55 questions presented in this part.

For example, if you answered 40 questions correctly, your raw score would be 40.

2. Converting Raw Score to Scaled Score

Once you've computed your raw score, the ensuing step is to transform it into a scaled score. The scaled score is extrapolated from the raw score through a procedure called equating, which compensates for any disparity in difficulty across different exam versions. The College Board provides a conversion chart to aid you in determining your scaled score based on your raw score. While the conversion chart may show slight deviations year over year, the primary process stays consistent. To transform your raw score to a scaled score, you can employ the conversion chart provided by the College Board for the specific exam year. For instance, applying a hypothetical conversion chart, a raw score of 40 might equate to a scaled score of 65.

After you've ascertained your scaled score for the Multiple Choice segment, you can compute the final score for this part by multiplying the scaled score by the percentage weight of the segment. Since Section I - Part A contributes 40% to the total exam score, you would multiply your scaled score by 0.4.

Using the previous example, if your scaled score is 65, your final score for Section I - Part A would be:

65 (scaled score) × 0.4 (section weight) = 26

In this example, your final score for the Multiple Choice section would be 26.

Keep in mind that this final score represents only a portion of your total AP European History Exam score. You should combine the final scores for all sections to calculate your overall exam score.

Part B: Short Answer Question(SAQ)

The SAQs section is made up of three questions, with an overall time constraint of 40 minutes. The questions are intended to span a broad spectrum of historical periods and themes, ensuring you get a chance to showcase your understanding of diverse areas of European history. The first pair of questions are mandatory and spotlight periods 2-7, while the third question presents a choice between two options, each covering a distinct time period (Question 3: periods 1-4 and Question 4: periods 5-8). This choice empowers you to pick the question that aligns best with your expertise and interests.

The SAQs section is designed to evaluate several crucial skills required for studying and interpreting history.

The primary goals of this segment encompass the following:
1. Critical Thinking

Critical thinking is an invaluable ability for historians, enabling them to assess evidence, decipher historical incidents, and formulate compelling arguments based on their analysis. In the SAQs, you'll be required to showcase your critical thinking prowess by evaluating the dependability and pertinence of historical sources, challenging the premises and viewpoints of historians, and amalgamating diverse evidence to construct cogent arguments.

2. Source Analysis

Analyzing historical sources is a fundamental skill for any student of history. The SAQs will necessitate you to analyze diverse primary and secondary sources, including but not limited to textual documents, images, graphs, and maps. Proficient source analysis involves interpreting the source's content, assessing the author's or creator's reliability and viewpoint, and placing the source within a specific historical framework. By refining this skill, you'll be better prepared to comprehend the intricacies and subtleties of historical evidence.

3. Historiographical Understanding

Historiography pertains to the analysis of historical writing and the methodologies adopted by historians to explain the past. A robust comprehension of historiography is critical for the SAQs, as it allows you to engage with the diverse interpretations and debates that inform our perception of history. Cultivating historiographical understanding involves acquainting yourself with the works of distinguished historians, recognizing the strengths and shortcomings of their contentions, and being competent in articulating the repercussions of their interpretations for the broader study of history.

4. Argumentation and Synthesis

The ability to construct coherent and persuasive arguments is a vital skill for any historian. In the SAQs, you will be required to create arguments based on historical evidence, interpretations, and your own critical analysis. Effective argumentation involves synthesizing diverse pieces of information, establishing clear connections between your evidence and your claims, and presenting your ideas in a logical, organized manner. By cultivating this ability, you will be equipped to articulate your comprehension of history proficiently and showcase your aptitude for critical and analytical thinking.

5. Writing and Communication

Lucid and efficient communication is paramount for SAQs, as it helps you articulate your thoughts and arguments in a manner easily comprehended by your readers. Robust writing skills are necessary to present your analysis, interpretations, and arguments in a succinct and persuasive fashion. To hone this skill, practice writing with clarity and brevity, ensuring your ideas are systematically arranged and backed by suitable evidence. Additionally, pay heed to grammar, punctuation, and syntax, as these elements augment the overall clarity and persuasiveness of your writing.

When gearing up for the SAQs section of the AP European History Examination, it's essential to comprehend and develop the skills needed to excel in this segment of the test.

Types of Questions in the SAQs Section

Some common types of questions you may encounter in this section include the following:

1. Source-Based Questions

These questions necessitate you to analyze primary or secondary sources, like textual documents, visuals, graphs, or maps. You'll be required to assess the credibility and perspective of a source, contextualizing it within its specific historical scenario. This type of question tests your capability to interact with historical data and reach conclusions based on your evaluation.

2. Historiographical Questions

Questions in this category delve into the analysis of historical scripts and the methodologies historians use to decipher the past. You may be required to involve yourself with prominent historians' work, critique their argument's strength and weaknesses, or express the impact their interpretations bear on the wider scope of historical studies. This question type scrutinizes your grasp on historiography and your ability to critically analyze historical interpretations.

3. Thematic Questions

Thematic questions invite you to delve into specific themes or topics within European histories, like political, economic, social, or cultural developments. These questions require you to analyze patterns and trends, make connections between historical incidents, and provide evidence to substantiate your conclusions. This type of question assesses your ability to synthesize information and draw links between different historical incidents and developments.

4. Comparative Questions

These queries ask you to juxtapose historical episodes, advancements, or viewpoints from various eras or areas. You may be expected to highlight parallels and disparities, assess the relevance of these juxtapositions, or elaborate on the factors that led to the similarities or differences. This type of question assesses your ability to analyze historical incidents and developments within a broader comparative framework.

5. Period-Based Questions

These questions focus on specific historical periods and require you to demonstrate your understanding of the key events, developments, and trends that characterized these eras. During the exam, you may encounter questions that require you to scrutinize the reasons or aftermath of a particular event, deliberate on the influences that facilitated change or stability during a distinct era or appraise the importance of a specific historical progression. This question assesses your knowledge of European history and your ability to analyze historical events and developments within a specific chronological framework.

Scoring for Short Answer Questions (SAQs)

Each SAQ comprises 3 questions, all of which must be answered. The first couple of questions will be mandatory, while the third question will offer a choice between two options, each concentrating on a different era. Each SAQ is scored on a scale of 0 to 3 points, which implies that the total potential score for this segment is 9 points.

Here is the breakdown of the scoring rubric for each SAQ:

1. **Thesis/Claim (1 point):** To earn this point, you must provide a clear and coherent thesis or claim that directly addresses the question prompt. Your thesis should be specific and effectively convey your response's central argument or main idea. Vague, overly general, or restated prompts will not earn this point.

2. **Evidence (1 point):** You must support your thesis or claim with accurate and relevant historical evidence to earn this point. This evidence can come from your knowledge of the course material or from the provided primary or secondary sources (if applicable). Your evidence should be specific, clearly connected to your thesis, and effectively demonstrate your understanding of the historical context.

3. **Analysis (1 point):** To earn this point, you must analyze the evidence you have provided and explain how it supports your thesis or claim. Your analysis should demonstrate your ability to think critically about the historical context, make connections between different events or developments, and draw meaningful conclusions. Merely describing the evidence without analyzing its significance will not earn this point.

Section II

1. Document-Based Question (DBQ)

You will be allocated 60 minutes to complete the DBQ, which encompasses a 15-
minute reading phase. During this reading phase, you should peruse the
documents, jot down notes, and analyze their content in preparation for drafting
your essay. After the reading phase, you will have 45 minutes to pen down your
response.

The DBQ will consist of a single question that asks you to analyze a historical
issue, event, or development within periods 3-8. The question will typically
require you to assess the significance, causes, or effects of the topic at hand or to
evaluate the validity of different historical interpretations or perspectives. In
some cases, the question may ask you to compare and contrast different
viewpoints or developments within the specified time period.

To help you construct your response, you will be given seven documents related
to the question prompt.

These documents may include the following:

1. Written Texts

Letters, speeches, essays, and other primary and secondary sources such as
scholarly articles or historical analyses.

2. Visual Materials

Paintings, photographs, or other visual artworks provide insight into the
historical period or issue being discussed.

3. Maps

Geographical representations help contextualize events, developments, or perspectives within the broader historical context.

4. Graphs and Charts

Quantitative data representations, such as population figures, economic data, or other statistical information, can help support your argument.

The documents will be diverse in their perspectives and viewpoints, representing various aspects of the historical issue, event, or development being discussed. It is your task to analyze these documents critically and use them as evidence to build your argument.

Skills Assessed

The Document-Based Question (DBQ) is designed to assess a range of historical thinking skills and content knowledge.

The following skills are particularly emphasized in this section of the AP European History Exam:

1. Source Analysis

You must be able to closely read and analyze primary and secondary sources to understand their content, context, and perspective. This includes identifying the author's point of view, purpose, and intended audience and recognizing potential biases or limitations in the source material.

2. Historical Contextualization

You should be able to situate the provided documents within the broader historical context of the time period and issue under examination. This requires a solid understanding of key historical events, trends, and developments and an awareness of the connections between different aspects of the historical narrative.

3. Use of Evidence

The DBQ requires you to use the provided documents as evidence to support your argument. This involves selecting relevant evidence from the documents, explaining its significance, and incorporating it effectively into your essay to strengthen your overall argument.

4. Thesis Development and Argumentation

You need to develop a clear and well-argued thesis statement that directly addresses the question prompt and provides a roadmap for your essay. Your thesis should be supported by a logical and coherent argument, which is constructed using evidence from the provided documents and your own historical knowledge.

5. Synthesis and Interpretation

The DBQ tests your ability to synthesize and interpret a diverse range of source material, drawing connections between different documents and perspectives to construct a nuanced understanding of the historical issue, event, or development under examination. This requires critical thinking skills and recognizing and reconciling conflicting viewpoints or interpretations.

6. Comparison and Contrast

Some DBQ questions may ask you to compare and contrast different perspectives, events, or developments within the specified time period. This requires you to identify similarities and differences between the subjects under comparison and to analyze the significance of these similarities and differences for your overall argument.

7. Causation and Effect

The DBQ may require you to assess the causes or effects of a particular historical issue, event, or development. This involves identifying and analyzing the various factors that contributed to the phenomenon under examination and evaluating their relative importance or impact.

8. Continuity and Change Over Time

You may be asked to analyze the ways in which a particular historical issue, event, or development changed or remained constant over time. This requires you to identify continuity and change patterns and explain their significance for understanding the broader historical context.

By mastering these skills, you will be well-prepared to tackle the DBQ section of the AP European History Exam and to demonstrate your ability to think critically and analytically about historical issues, events, and developments.

Scoring and Rubric for Document-Based Question (DBQ)

The DBQ section comprises 25% of your total exam score, making it a significant component of the test. It is scored using a rubric that evaluates your response based on a set of specific criteria. The DBQ rubric generally has a total of seven points, each focusing on a different aspect of your essay.

Below is a brief overview of the scoring criteria:

1. **Thesis and Argument Development (1 point):** To earn this point, you must create a clear, historically defensible, and well-argued thesis statement that directly addresses the question prompt. The thesis statement must be brief and precise, outlining the key arguments that will be presented in the remainder of the essay.

2. **Contextualization (1 point):** To earn this point, you need to provide a broader historical context for the specific topic you are discussing. This involves situating your argument within the larger historical trends, events, or developments relevant to the question prompt.

3. **Evidence from the Documents (2 points):** You can earn up to two points for effectively using evidence from the provided documents to support your argument. The first point is awarded for using evidence from at least three documents, while the second point is awarded for using evidence from six or seven documents.

4. **Sourcing the Documents (2 points):** You can earn up to two points for your ability to analyze and evaluate the sources of the documents. This involves discussing the author's point of view, purpose, historical context, or audience for at least three documents. One point is awarded for analyzing the sourcing of three documents, and the second point is awarded for analyzing the sourcing of four documents.

5. **Outside Evidence (1 point):** To earn this point, you must bring in additional historical evidence beyond the documents provided. This

outside evidence should be relevant and effectively used to support your thesis and argument.

To calculate the weighted score for the DBQ:

Multiply the points you earned by the percentage it contributes to the overall exam score.

For example, if you earned 6 points on the DBQ, your weighted score would be: 6 (points earned) x 0.25 (DBQ's contribution to overall exam score) = 1.5

---

2. Long Essay Question (LEQ)

Long Essay Question The Long Essay Question (LEQ) is designed to assess your ability to explain and analyze significant issues in European history while developing a coherent argument supported by historical evidence. When you receive the LEQ prompt, you will be given three essay choices, each focusing on the same theme and skill but in different time periods.

The options will be divided as follows:
- **Option 1:** Periods 1-3
- **Option 2:** Periods 4-6
- **Option 3:** Periods 7-8

You are required to choose one of these prompts and compose a coherent essay within a 40-minute time frame. These time periods cover a broad range of European history, enabling you to demonstrate your understanding and analysis of various historical events, trends, and themes. By choosing an essay prompt that aligns with your strengths and areas of interest, you can maximize your chances of success on the LEQ portion of the AP European History exam.

Skills Assessed

The LEQ assesses various skills that are crucial for success in the AP European History course and the exam.

These skills include:

1. Historical Argumentation

Constructing a persuasive argument is a foundational skill in historical writing. You need to develop a clear, concise thesis statement that responds directly to the prompt and sets the stage for your essay. Your argument should be supported by well-organized paragraphs with clear topic sentences that relate back to your thesis. Moreover, your essay should be logically structured, ensuring that each paragraph builds on the previous one to advance your argument.

2. Use of Evidence

Providing specific historical evidence is crucial for substantiating your argument. This includes incorporating primary and secondary sources and your own knowledge of European history to support your claims. You should use diverse evidence types, such as documents, images, graphs, or maps, to create a well-rounded argument.

3. Contextualization

Placing your argument within the broader historical context is essential for demonstrating your understanding of European history. This means explaining how your argument relates to larger historical trends, events, or developments within the relevant time period. By providing context, you can show your ability to connect your argument to the larger historical narrative and explain its significance.

4. Synthesis

Synthesizing information from various sources and connecting different historical themes, periods, and concepts is an essential skill for historians. In the LEQ, you should demonstrate your ability to draw meaningful connections between different aspects of European history, revealing a comprehensive understanding of the subject matter. Synthesis can strengthen your argument and provide deeper insights into the historical topic being discussed.

5. Continuity and Change Over Time

Analyzing continuity and change over time is a key aspect of historical thinking. This skill involves identifying patterns of persistence or transformation in historical events, developments, or trends. In the LEQ, you must evaluate the significance of these patterns and explain the reasons behind them, demonstrating your ability to think critically about historical change.

6. Comparison

Comparing and contrasting different historical events, developments, or processes is another essential skill for historians. In the LEQ, you may be asked to identify similarities and differences between various historical topics, explain their significance, and assess the reasons behind them. Refining your comparative abilities can facilitate a more profound comprehension of the intricacies and subtleties of European history.

7. Causation

Grasping cause-and-effect relationships in history is crucial for understanding the dynamics of historical events and developments. In the LEQ, you should be able to identify and analyze the causes and consequences of various historical phenomena and explain the reasons behind them. This skill requires you to think critically about the interconnectedness of historical events, helping you to develop a more sophisticated understanding of European history.

Scoring and Rubric for Long Essay Question (LEQ)

The evaluation method for the Long Essay Question (LEQ) on the AP European History exam involves using a rubric. This rubric examines your ability to create a thesis-driven argument using historical evidence. The LEQ accounts for 15% of your total exam score.

The rubric for the LEQ has six points, which are as follows:

1. **Thesis/Claim (0-1 point):** This point is awarded for creating a clear and defendable thesis statement that answers the prompt and outlines the main points of your argument.
2. **Contextualization (0-1 point):** This point is awarded for providing historical context relevant to the prompt and demonstrating an understanding of historical events and processes connected to the topic.
3. **Evidence (0-2 points):**
   a. **Evidence Beyond the Documents (0-1 points):** This point is earned by using relevant historical evidence that goes beyond the provided documents or sources.

b. **Evidence from the Documents (0-1 point):** This point is earned by accurately using the documents provided in the prompt to support your argument.
4. **Analysis and Reasoning (0-2 points):**
   a. **Targeted Skill (0-1 point):** This point is earned by demonstrating an understanding of the historical thinking skill assessed in the prompt.
   b. **Complexity (0-1 point):** This point is earned by demonstrating a nuanced understanding of the historical issue or topic.

To calculate your score:

Multiply your raw score by 0.15. For example, if you earned 4 points on the LEQ, your weighted score would be 4 * 0.15 = 0.6.

Your total exam score is calculated by adding the weighted scores from each section: Weighted Multiple Choice Score + Weighted Short Answer Score + Weighted DBQ Score + Weighted LEQ Score. For example, if your weighted scores were 17.6 (Multiple Choice), 1.4 (Short Answer), 1.25 (DBQ), and 0.6 (LEQ), your total exam score would be 17.6 + 1.4 + 1.25 + 0.6 = 20.85.

The College Board uses specific cut-off points to determine your final AP score (on a scale of 1 to 5), which varies from year to year based on the difficulty of the exam and the performance of all test-takers. A score of 3 is considered passing, while a score of 4 or 5 is considered high enough to earn college credit or advanced placement at many institutions.

To succeed on the AP European History exam, it is essential to understand how to earn points and calculate your score. Focusing on each section's requirements and maximizing your performance can improve your chances of achieving a high score and earning college credit.

STRATEGIES TO ANSWERING THE MULTIPLE-CHOICE QUESTIONS

To perform well on the AP European History exam, particularly the multiple-choice questions (MCQ) section, it is crucial to devise effective strategies.

Here are some key approaches to optimize your score:

1. Read the Question Carefully

Reading the question carefully is the first and most important step in answering MCQs for the AP European History exam. If the question is fully understood, your chances of selecting the accurate answer increase substantially.

• Detect Key Words and Expressions

While reading the question, pay close attention to keywords and phrases that help you understand its main focus. Keywords might include names of historical figures, events, concepts, or time periods. By identifying these keywords, you can quickly establish the context of the question and recall relevant information from your studies. This will aid you in making more judicious decisions while reviewing the possible answers.

For instance, contemplate the question below:

"Which option most precisely represents the role of the printing press in spreading the Protestant Reformation in the 16th century?"

The pivotal words in this query are **"printing press," "Protestant Reformation,"** and **"16th century."** Recognizing these keywords can help you comprehend that the question is investigating the correlation between the printing press and the Protestant Reformation during the 16th century. This understanding will facilitate the recollection of pertinent information about the printing press's role during the Reformation, helping you in evaluating the possible answers.

• Understand the Context of the Question

After identifying the keywords, it's crucial to understand the context of the question. This means considering the time period, location, and historical events or figures mentioned. A solid grasp of the background can improve your ability to assess the response options, thereby raising the odds of identifying the correct response.

Taking the example above, comprehending the context implies recognizing that the question pertains to the Protestant Reformation in the 16th century. This comprehension lets you recall specific elements about the influence of the printing press in disseminating ideas, which, in turn, impacted the spread of the Reformation.

By reading the question carefully and focusing on both keywords and context, you set a strong foundation for choosing the correct answer. This strategy helps you recall relevant information and accurately assess the answer choices, ultimately increasing your chances of success on the AP European History exam's MCQ section.

2. Process of Elimination

The process of elimination is a critical strategy for answering MCQs on the AP European History exam. It involves eliminating incorrect or less likely answer choices to narrow down your options and increase your chances of selecting the correct answer.

• Eliminate Clearly Incorrect Answers

Start by reviewing each answer choice and eliminating any clearly incorrect or irrelevant options. This strategy involves identifying options that are factually wrong, refer to events or figures unrelated to the question's context, or are otherwise implausible. By discarding such options, you lessen your potential responses, thus increasing the probability of selecting the right one.

For instance, if a question deals with the causes of the French Revolution, and one of the answer choices mentions the American Civil War, you can readily discard that choice because it does not pertain to the question's context.

• Look for Answer Choices that are Similar, and Eliminate One or Both if They Contradict Each Other

Sometimes, two answer choices may seem very similar or have overlapping information. In such cases, carefully consider the differences between the options and eliminate one or both if they contradict or cannot be correct. This strategy helps you further narrow down your choices and focus on the most likely correct answer.

For example, if two answer choices discuss the impact of the Congress of Vienna but offer opposing outcomes, it is likely that one of these options needs to be corrected. By comparing and evaluating these similar answer choices, you can eliminate the less plausible option and increase your chances of choosing the correct answer.

• Identify the Most Likely Correct Answer After Narrowing Down Choices

After eliminating the clearly incorrect and contradictory answer choices, you should be left with fewer options to consider. At this point, employ your subject knowledge and the question's context to identify the likeliest correct answer. Remember, the right answer might not always seem apparent; meticulously analyze the remaining choices and select the one that best aligns with the question's information and your understanding of the topic.

By employing the process of elimination, you can effectively reduce the number of answer choices you need to consider and increase your chances of selecting the correct answer on the AP European History exam's MCQ section.

3. Analyze Answer Choices

Analyzing answer choices is another crucial strategy for tackling MCQs on the AP European History exam. This approach involves carefully examining each answer choice in relation to the question, historical context, and themes. Doing so can allow for a more informed decision when selecting the right answer.

• Consider Historical Context and Themes

When evaluating answer choices, think about the historical context and themes related to the question. This includes considering the time period, location, events, and figures mentioned in the question. By incorporating this contextual knowledge, you can better understand the answer choices and identify the most appropriate option.

Assume a question explores the significance of religion in the Thirty Years' War. Ponder the wider context of the conflict, like the strife between the Catholics and Protestants within the Holy Roman Empire. This understanding can help you ascertain which answer aligns best with the historical context and themes.

• Look for Patterns or Connections Between Answer Choices

When analyzing answer choices, search for patterns or connections that may help you identify the correct answer. This might include recognizing similarities between choices, understanding how they relate to the question's context, or noting any recurring themes. Identifying these patterns or connections can provide additional insight when selecting the correct answer.

If the bourgeoisie's role in the French Revolution is highlighted in more than one option, it could suggest that the bourgeoisie's role is crucial to the question. Recognizing this pattern could guide your decision-making process.

• Watch for Answer Choices with Extreme Language or Absolutes

Be wary of answer choices that use extreme terms or absolutes, such as **"always," "never,"** or **"only."** These options can be deceptive and need to be validated. History is complex, and such definitive statements are rarely accurate. When evaluating answer choices, be skeptical of options that use extreme language and consider whether these assertions are truly accurate within the context of the question.

For example, suppose an answer choice states that the Industrial Revolution **"completely eliminated"** the agrarian lifestyle. In such a situation, doubt the accuracy of this statement as it's unlikely that the Industrial Revolution had such a profound impact on agriculture.

By critically scrutinizing each potential answer, you can select the correct answer more efficiently and avoid common mistakes such as choosing an option because it appears correct or picking an incorrect answer because it seems attractive. This method reduces the likelihood of selecting a wrong answer and increases your chances of achieving a higher score.

4. Prioritize Primary Source-Based Questions

Primary source-based questions are essential to the AP European History exam's MCQ section. These questions require you to analyze excerpts from historical documents, such as speeches, letters, or laws, and use your knowledge of the context to answer the question.

To effectively tackle primary source-based questions, prioritize the following steps:

a. Read and Analyze the Primary Source Excerpt

Begin by carefully reading the primary source excerpt provided with the question. Focus on understanding the main ideas, arguments, or points of view expressed in the source. Pay attention to any critical words, phrases, or references that enhance your comprehension of the source's content and intent. When scrutinizing the source, it's beneficial to account for the author's viewpoint, inclinations, or motives.

b. Use Contextual Knowledge to Understand the Source's Significance

After analyzing the primary source excerpt, use your knowledge of the historical context to understand its significance. Reflect on the era, locale, events, and personalities associated with the source, and ponder how the source correlates with the broader historical narrative. This contextual comprehension can assist you in linking the source and the question, ultimately directing you toward the right answer.

For instance, if the primary source is a speech by Martin Luther condemning the Catholic Church, you should contemplate the backdrop of the Protestant Reformation and Luther's part in contesting the Church's dominance.

c. Pick an Answer that Matches the Source and Your Comprehension of the Historical Context

Finally, scrutinize the options and select the one that best corresponds with both the primary source and your comprehension of the historical context. Remember, the right answer should not only be corroborated by the source but also accurately mirror the overarching historical themes and events related to the question.

Primary source-based questions are a key component of the AP European History exam, and analyzing primary sources is essential to earning a high score. By focusing on the primary source excerpt, contextual knowledge, and related themes, you can identify the most appropriate answer to each question.

5. Practice Educated Guessing

In the MCQ section of the AP European History exam, you may encounter questions for which you need clarification on the correct answer. In such cases, practicing educated guessing can be a valuable strategy. Educated guessing involves using your knowledge of the topic and logical reasoning to make an informed decision, even if you need more confidence in your choice.

Here are some tips for practicing educated guessing:

- If uncertain, make an informed guess based on your knowledge of the topic. Recall related information from your studies, and use this knowledge to evaluate the answer choices. Even when your certainty in your choice wavers, using pertinent information as a basis for your guess can enhance your chances of selecting the correct response.

For example, if a question probes the Enlightenment's effect on the French Revolution, you may not recall intricate details, but you may remember that the Enlightenment advocated for liberty, equality, and democracy. Armed with this knowledge, you can make an enlightened guess by picking the answer that best fits these ideologies.

• Avoid random guessing

Guessing blindly is not a viable strategy, as it does not enhance your chances of choosing the correct answer. Always base your informed guess on logical reasoning or your knowledge of the topic. Consider the context of the question, the answer options, and any patterns or connections that might help guide your decision. By engaging in careful reasoning, you increase the probability of choosing the correct answer, even when uncertain.

It is crucial to remember that incorrect AP European History exam answers are not penalized. Consequently, when unsure, make an educated guess rather than leaving the question unanswered. By utilizing your subject knowledge and logical reasoning, you can boost your chances of performing well on the exam's multiple-choice section.

6. Manage Time Effectively

Effectively managing your time is essential for success on the MCQ section of the AP European History exam. The exam typically consists of 55 MCQs; you have 55 minutes to complete this section. Time management helps you maintain a steady pace and ensures that you have enough time to answer all questions.

Consider these helpful suggestions for efficiently managing your time while taking the exam:

• Allocate a specific duration for each question.

Divide the total time available (55 minutes) by the number of questions (55) to ascertain how much time you should devote to each question. In this scenario, you should allocate about 1 minute per question. Although it's not necessary to strictly adhere to this time limit for every question, having a general guideline can help maintain a steady rhythm throughout the test.

• Refrain from allocating too much time to a single question; progress to the next and return later if required.

If you find a specific question challenging, don't waste time on it. Instead, move to the next question and, if time allows, return to the difficult one. Spending too much time on one question could make you fall behind schedule and leave other questions unanswered. Bear in mind that every question carries equal weight, so it's preferable to answer more questions, even if some are informed guesses, rather than concentrating excessively on a single challenging question.

• Stay aware of the remaining time and adjust your speed accordingly

Regularly monitor the remaining time to ensure you're on track to complete the exam within the set time. If you find yourself needing extra time, adjust your pace to ensure you can address all questions. Conversely, if you find you're moving too rapidly, slow down to allocate more time to each question, making sure you thoroughly consider each answer choice.

By effectively managing your time during the MCQ section of the AP European History exam, you can maintain a steady pace and increase your chances of answering all questions within the allotted time. This strategy helps you maximize your score by ensuring that you have the opportunity to consider and answer every question on the exam.

7. Answer Every Question

Answering every AP European History exam question is an important strategy for maximizing your score. As there are no deductions for wrong answers, attempting all questions—even those you're unsure of—improves your chances of gaining points.

Here are some guidelines for ensuring you address every question on the test:

• There is no penalty for incorrect answers on the AP European History exam

The AP European History exam, unlike other exams, does not deduct points for incorrect answers. This means that you should always make an effort to answer every question, even if you are not confident in your choice. By attempting all questions, you increase your chances of earning points and improving your overall score.

- **Answer all questions, even if you are unsure, to maximize your chances of earning points**

Remember to practice educated guessing when faced with a question you're uncertain about. Use your knowledge of the topic and logical reasoning to make an informed decision, even if you need more confidence in your choice. By answering all questions, even those you're unsure of, you increase the likelihood of earning points and improving your score.

- **Be Mindful of the Time Remaining**

As you progress through the MCQ section, periodically check the time remaining to ensure that you are on track to complete the exam within the allotted time. If you find you require more time to answer all questions, adjust your speed to make sure you can respond to every query. If time is running out and you still have unanswered questions, make quick, educated guesses for those remaining to maximize your chances of earning points.

By answering every question on the AP European History exam, you can make the most of the scoring system and increase your chances of earning points. This strategy, combined with effective time management and other test-taking techniques, will help you maximize your score and succeed on the exam's MCQ section.

8. Practice, Practice, Practice

Practicing is essential for success on the AP European History exam, particularly for the MCQ section. Regular practice helps you become familiar with the format, content, and structure of the questions, and it allows you to refine your test-taking strategies over time.

Here are some tips for incorporating the practice into your exam preparation:
- **Use Practice Exams**

Utilize available practice exams, such as those provided by the College Board, textbooks, or other reputable sources, to familiarize yourself with the MCQ format. Practice exams help you understand the types of questions you'll encounter, the way questions are phrased, and the general structure of the test.

Regular practice will also help you identify your strengths and weaknesses, allowing you to focus your studies on areas that need improvement.

• Review Your Answers and Learn From Your Mistakes

After completing practice exams, thoroughly review your answers to understand where you made mistakes and why. Analyze both correct and incorrect answers to identify patterns in your reasoning or gaps in your knowledge. By learning from your mistakes, you can adjust your test-taking strategies and improve your performance on future practice exams and the actual test.

• Track Your Progress and Adjust Your Strategies

As you complete practice exams, track your progress by noting your scores and the types of questions you consistently struggle with. Use this information to identify areas where you need to improve your knowledge or test-taking strategies. Adjusting your approach based on your performance will help you fine-tune your skills and increase your chances of success on the exam.

By practicing regularly, reviewing your answers, and tracking your progress, you can effectively prepare for the MCQ section of the AP European History exam. Engaging in consistent practice helps you become more comfortable with the test format, improve your test-taking strategies, and ultimately achieve a higher score on the exam.

By incorporating these strategies into your exam preparation, you can develop the skills and confidence needed to succeed on the MCQ section of the AP European History exam.

SAMPLE QUESTIONS AND ANSWER

1. Which Renaissance intellectual movement focused on the study of the classical texts, values, and styles of Greece and Rome?
    A) Neoplatonism
    B) Scholasticism
    C) Humanism
    D) Romanticism

Answer: C

2. Who was the English king or queen who left the Catholic Church and started the Church of England?

   A) Elizabeth I
   B) Henry VII
   C) Henry VIII
   D) James I

Answer: C

3. Which 17th-century event marked the beginning of the modern concept of a constitutional monarchy in England?

   A) The English Civil War
   B) The Glorious Revolution
   C) The Restoration
   D) The Gunpowder Plot

Answer: B

4. Which French philosopher is best known for his idea of "separation of powers," which influenced the way democratic governments work today?

   A) Jean-Jacques Rousseau
   B) René Descartes
   C) Voltaire
   D) Montesquieu

Answer: D

5. The Industrial Revolution led to significant urbanization. Which of the following was NOT a direct consequence of urbanization?

   A) Overcrowding and poor living conditions
   B) The growth of factories and industry
   C) The development of public education systems

D) A decline in agricultural production

Answer: D

6. Who was the German philosopher that co-authored the Communist Manifesto with Friedrich Engels and heavily criticized capitalism?
   A) Immanuel Kant
   B) Georg Wilhelm Friedrich Hegel
   C) Karl Marx
   D) Max Weber

Answer: C

7. Which event was a direct cause of World War I?
   A) The assassination of Archduke Franz Ferdinand
   B) The Treaty of Versailles
   C) The sinking of the Lusitania
   D) The Zimmerman Telegram

Answer: A

8. What was the primary purpose of the Marshall Plan?
   A) To rebuild war-torn Europe after World War II
   B) To provide economic aid to the Soviet Union
   C) To establish a military alliance between the United States and Western European countries
   D) To create a free trade zone in Europe

Answer: A

9. Which event marked the symbolic end of the Cold War?
   A) The Cuban Missile Crisis
   B) The fall of the Berlin Wall
   C) The dissolution of the Soviet Union

D) The signing of the Helsinki Accords

Answer: B

10. What has been a major challenge for the European Union in recent years?
   A) The rise of nationalism and populism
   B) The decline in global trade
   C) The resurgence of communism
   D) The threat of invasion by non-European powers

Answer: A

11. Which artistic style is most closely associated with the Romantic movement of the 19th century?
   A) Baroque
   B) Realism
   C) Neoclassicism
   D) Gothic Revival

Answer: D

12. The Scramble for Africa refers to:
   A) The migration of African peoples across the continent
   B) The competition between European powers to colonize Africa
   C) The struggle for independence in African countries
   D) The efforts of African nations to industrialize

Answer: B

13. Who was the main architect of Italian unification?
   A) Giuseppe Mazzini
   B) Giuseppe Garibaldi
   C) Camillo di Cavour
   D) Victor Emmanuel II

Answer: C

14. Which scientific theory, developed during the Scientific Revolution, replaced the geocentric model of the universe?
    A) Newton's laws of motion
    B) The heliocentric model
    C) The laws of thermodynamics
    D) The theory of relativity

Answer: B

15. The Treaty of Tordesillas, signed in 1494, was an agreement between:
    A) England and France
    B) Spain and Portugal
    C) The Holy Roman Empire and the Papacy
    D) The Ottoman Empire and the Safavid Empire

Answer: B

16. The Peace of Westphalia, which ended the Thirty Years' War in 1648, established the principle of:
    A) Popular sovereignty
    B) Separation of church and state
    C) Cuius regio, eius religio
    D) Balance of power

Answer: C

17. Which of the following is NOT a characteristic of the Enlightenment?
    A) Emphasis on reason and rational thought
    B) A focus on individual rights and liberties
    C) Advocacy for absolute monarchy
    D) Belief in the power of education and knowledge

Answer: C

18. Which event is considered the start of the French Revolution?
    A) The execution of Louis XVI
    B) The fall of the Bastille
    C) The Tennis Court Oath
    D) The Reign of Terror

Answer: B

19. Which of these was NOT a reason why the Russian Revolution happened?
    A) Widespread economic inequality
    B) The Russian defeat in the Russo-Japanese War
    C) The assassination of Tsar Alexander II
    D) The impact of World War I on Russia

Answer: C

20. Which of the following was NOT a major factor contributing to the rise of fascism in Europe during the interwar period?
    A) The economic crisis of the Great Depression
    B) The resentment caused by the Treaty of Versailles
    C) The success of socialist revolutions in other countries
    D) The fear of communism

Answer: C

21. The European Recovery Program, aimed at rebuilding the economies of Western European countries after World War II, is also known as:
    A) The Marshall Plan
    B) The Truman Doctrine
    C) The Schuman Plan
    D) The Morgenthau Plan

Answer: A

22. Which European organization was established in 1957 by the Treaty of Rome?
   A) The Council of Europe
   B) The European Coal and Steel Community
   C) The European Economic Community
   D) The Western European Union

Answer: C

23. The main goal of the Congress of Vienna (1814-1815) was to:
   A) Establish a balance of power in Europe
   B) Punish France for the Napoleonic Wars
   C) Support the spread of liberalism and nationalism
   D) Encourage industrialization and economic growth

Answer: A

24. The policy of appeasement was most closely associated with which British Prime Minister?
   A) Winston Churchill
   B) Neville Chamberlain
   C) Clement Attlee
   D) David Lloyd George

Answer: B

25. The Cuban Missile Crisis was a confrontation between which two superpowers?
   A) United States and Soviet Union
   B) United States and China
   C) Soviet Union and China

D) Soviet Union and United Kingdom

Answer: A

26. What was the purpose of the Warsaw Pact?
    A) To provide a mutual defense alliance for Eastern European countries under Soviet influence
    B) To establish an economic union between Eastern European countries
    C) To promote the spread of communism in Western Europe
    D) To negotiate the peaceful end of the Cold War

Answer: A

27. The European Union was officially established by the following:
    A) Treaty of Maastricht
    B) Treaty of Rome
    C) Treaty of Lisbon
    D) Schengen Agreement

Answer: A

28. The Eurozone crisis was primarily caused by:
    A) A decline in global trade
    B) High levels of government debt in some European countries
    C) A decrease in European industrial production
    D) The expansion of the European Union

Answer: B

29. Which event significantly increased the number of refugees and migrants entering Europe in the mid-2010s?
    A) The Syrian Civil War
    B) The collapse of the Soviet Union
    C) The global financial crisis

D) The Eurozone crisis

Answer: A

30. The Schengen Agreement primarily concerns:
    A) The free movement of goods within the European Union
    B) The establishment of a single European currency
    C) The abolition of border controls between participating European countries
    D) The establishment of a European defense alliance

Answer: C

31. Which European country voted to leave the European Union in a 2016 referendum?
    A) France
    B) United Kingdom
    C) Italy
    D) Greece

Answer: B

32. The rise of nationalism and populism in Europe has been most closely associated with:
    A) The success of far-left political parties
    B) The rejection of globalization and multiculturalism
    C) The growth of the European Union
    D) The decline of religion in European societies

Answer: B

33. The main goal of the Paris Agreement, adopted in 2015, is to:
    A) Combat global terrorism
    B) Address the European migration crisis
    C) Regulate international trade

D) Combat climate change and limit global temperature increases

Answer: D

34. Which European city is considered the de facto capital of the European Union, hosting several key institutions and agencies?
   A) Paris
   B) Berlin
   C) Brussels
   D) Vienna

Answer: C

35. The "Iron Curtain" was a term coined by Winston Churchill to describe the:
   A) Division of Europe between NATO and the Warsaw Pact countries
   B) Border between East and West Germany
   C) Period of political repression in the Soviet Union
   D) Military buildup between the United States and the Soviet Union during the Cold War

Answer: A

36. The policy of détente during the Cold War aimed to:
   A) Promote the spread of democracy in Eastern Europe
   B) Encourage the collapse of the Soviet Union
   C) Lessen the tensions between the US and the USSR and lower the chance that they will fight
   D) Increase military spending to pressure the Soviet Union

Answer: C

37. Which event marked the official end of the Soviet Union?
   A) The fall of the Berlin Wall
   B) The signing of the Helsinki Accords

C) The dissolution of the Soviet Union in 1991

D) The signing of the START Treaty

Answer: C

38. Which of the following is NOT a current challenge faced by the European Union?

A) The rise of nationalism and populism

B) Economic stagnation in some member states

C) The threat of invasion by non-European powers

D) Addressing climate change and environmental challenges

Answer: C

39. The concept of the "social contract" was most famously articulated by which Enlightenment philosopher?

A) John Locke

B) Jean-Jacques Rousseau

C) Montesquieu

D) Voltaire

Answer: B

40. Which of the following best describes the artistic style of the Baroque period?

A) A focus on order, symmetry, and classical themes

B) A rejection of religious themes in favor of secular subjects

C) An emphasis on emotion, drama, and grandeur

D) A simplistic, unadorned style that focused on everyday life

Answer: C

41. The 19th-century doctrine of "manifest destiny" most directly influenced which of the following?

A) British imperialism in Africa and Asia
B) German unification under Bismarck
C) Italian unification under Garibaldi
D) American westward expansion and territorial acquisitions

Answer: D

42. The period of European history known as the Belle Époque (1871-1914) was characterized by:
A) Rapid industrialization and urbanization
B) A flourishing of arts, culture, and scientific advancements
C) A decline in imperialism and colonialism
D) Political stability and the absence of major wars

Answer: B

43. After World War I, the Treaty of Versailles had which of the following effects on Germany?
A) It imposed severe financial reparations, territorial losses, and military restrictions, contributing to economic and political instability.
B) It allowed Germany to keep all of its pre-war territories but required significant military disarmament.
C) It forced Germany to join the League of Nations and adopt a democratic form of government.
D) It encouraged Germany to pursue a policy of appeasement and avoid future conflicts.

Answer: A

44. The Holocaust refers to:
A) The systematic genocide of approximately six million European Jews by Nazi Germany during World War II
B) Joseph Stalin's rule in the Soviet Union was marked by mass starvation and political repression

C) The mass deportations and forced labor of European civilians by Nazi Germany during World War II
D) The atomic bombs dropped on Hiroshima and Nagasaki caused a lot of damage and deaths

Answer: A

45. The "Domino Theory" was a Cold War-era belief that:
   A) If one country fell to communism, neighboring countries would also fall, like a row of dominoes
   B) The United States and the Soviet Union were on a path to mutually assured destruction
   C) The division of Europe into democratic and communist spheres would lead to a new world order
   D) The spread of communism could be contained through military and economic aid to threatened countries

Answer: A

46. The main goal of the Truman Doctrine was to:
   A) Contain the spread of communism by providing economic and military aid to threatened countries
   B) Establish a European defense alliance against Soviet aggression
   C) Promote the reunification of East and West Germany
   D) Encourage the spread of democracy in Eastern Europe

Answer: A

47. The Berlin Wall was erected in 1961 to:
   A) Separate the Soviet-controlled sector of Berlin from the other Allied-occupied sectors
   B) Mark the border between East and West Germany
   C) Prevent East Germans from fleeing to West Germany
   D) Establish a buffer zone between NATO and Warsaw Pact countries

Answer: C

48. Which of the following events marked the beginning of the end for the Soviet Union?
    A) The invasion of Afghanistan in 1979
    B) The signing of the Helsinki Accords in 1975
    C) The implementation of Gorbachev's policies of glasnost and perestroika in the 1980s
    D) The Sino-Soviet split in the 1960s

Answer: C

49. Which of the following is a key component of globalization in the late 20th and early 21st centuries?
    A) The decline of international trade
    B) The rise of nationalist and isolationist policies
    C) The increased interconnectedness of countries through economic, political, and cultural exchanges
    D) The reduction of environmental challenges due to international cooperation

Answer: C

50. One of the main challenges facing the European Union in the 21st century is:
    A) The potential expansion of the Eurozone
    B) The need for a common European language
    C) The rise of nationalist and populist movements that challenge the EU's values and goals
    D) The declining influence of the United States in European affairs

Answer: C

51. The economic system of mercantilism was most closely associated with:

A) The Age of Exploration and the establishment of European colonies around the world
B) The Industrial Revolution and the growth of capitalism
C) The Enlightenment and the promotion of free trade
D) The post-World War II era and the rise of the European Economic Community

Answer: A

52. The Edict of Nantes, issued in 1598, was significant because it:
   A) Established religious toleration between Catholics and Protestants in France
   B) Created a unified French state under the rule of an absolute monarch
   C) Led to the expulsion of the Huguenots from France
   D) Marked the beginning of French exploration and colonization in the Americas

Answer: A

53. The Glorious Revolution of 1688 in England resulted in:
   A) The establishment of a constitutional monarchy under William and Mary
   B) The restoration of the Stuart monarchy
   C) The end of religious conflict between Catholics and Protestants
   D) The beginning of England's imperial expansion

Answer: A

54. The Industrial Revolution began in which country?
   A) France
   B) Germany
   C) United Kingdom
   D) United States

Answer: C

55. The Congress System, also known as the Concert of Europe, was a diplomatic framework established after the Napoleonic Wars with the goal of:

    A) Maintaining a balance of power and preventing future wars in Europe
    B) Encouraging the spread of liberalism and nationalism
    C) Promoting economic cooperation and free trade among European nations
    D) Establishing a common European currency

Answer: A

MASTERING SHORT ANSWER QUESTIONS (SAQ)

Unlike DBQ and LEQ, which provide more space for topic exploration, the SAQ section requires students to demonstrate their understanding of historical events, themes, and concepts concisely, often within a restricted space or word count, making it crucial to develop effective strategies for responding to SAQs.

Keep in mind the following points:

1. Reading The Prompt Carefully

Reading the prompt carefully is crucial for understanding what the question is asking and for formulating an appropriate response.

Here are some steps to follow when reading the prompt:

Step 1: Identify The Specific Task or Task Required

Carefully examine the question to determine what it is asking you to do. Typical tasks include explaining, comparing, contrasting, or analyzing historical events or concepts. Keep an eye out for directive words in the prompt like **"evaluate,"** **"explain,"** **"compare,"** **"assess,"** or **"identify,"** that hint at the type of answer desired.

For instance, the prompt may state:

"Compare and contrast the political and economic structures of France and England during the 18th century."

In this scenario, the explicit task is to compare and contrast the systems of the two nations.

Step 2: Take Note of Historical Themes, Events, or Concepts Mentioned

As you read the prompt, mentally note any historical themes, events, or concepts mentioned. These will be crucial in formulating your response and providing appropriate evidence. Recognizing the specific historical context of the question will help you narrow your focus and select the most relevant information.

In the example prompt, the historical themes include political and economic systems, and the specific context is 18th-century France and England.

Step 3: Determine the Time Period or Context Being Addressed

Identify the time period, region, or particular historical context in which the question is set. This will help you select appropriate evidence and examples when crafting your response. Be mindful of any specific dates or events mentioned in the prompt.

In our example, the context is clearly defined as the 18th century. Knowing this will help you focus on the political and economic systems of France and England during that specific time period.

Step 4: Pay Attention to the Prompt's Structure

Examine the prompt for any hints about its structure or organization. Some questions may be multipart, requiring you to address several aspects of a topic. Be prepared to answer each part separately and ensure that your response is well-organized and coherent.

For instance, if the prompt reads, *"Evaluate the causes of the French Revolution and assess its impact on European politics,"* you would need to address both the causes and the impact in your response.

Step 5: Reread the Prompt

Prior to beginning your answer, take a moment to re-examine the prompt to confirm that you have a comprehensive comprehension of the inquiry and its specifications. Initially, it may be easy to miss significant details or misunderstandings, so verifying your understanding can ultimately save you time and energy.

2. Organize Your Thoughts

Before commencing your response, take a moment to organize your thoughts and ideas. This will aid in producing a well-ordered and coherent answer that addresses all elements of the prompt.

Listed below are a few recommended procedures to adhere to while structuring your ideas:

Step 1: Jot Down Key Ideas or Points Related to the Prompt

Quickly note down any relevant ideas, points, or evidence that comes to mind. This can include historical events, figures, concepts, or themes related to the question. This "brain dump" will help you focus your thoughts and identify the most important points to include in your response.

Step 2: Consider Any Relevant Historical Evidence or Examples

Think about specific historical evidence or examples that could support your response. This might include primary, secondary, or other types of evidence demonstrating your understanding of the topic. Make sure the evidence you choose is appropriate for the time period or context of the question.

Step 3: Outline a Brief Response Before Writing

Before you start writing your response, create a brief outline to guide your answer. This could be as basic as a few bullet points or a more elaborate roadmap of your primary points and supporting evidence. The objective is to create a clear and organized structure for your response, ensuring that you cover all aspects of the prompt and present your ideas in a coherent manner.

3. Be Concise and Specific

When answering SAQs, it's important to be concise and specific. Unlike DBQs and LEQs, which demand a more in-depth analysis, SAQs require you to showcase your understanding of historical events, themes, and concepts in a limited space or word count. To maximize your score, concentrate on delivering a clear, well-reasoned, and evidence-based answer that directly addresses the prompt.

Here are some suggestions for being concise and specific in your SAQ responses:

Tip 1: Answer Each Part of the Prompt Directly and Clearly

Make sure your response directly addresses each part of the prompt. Explicitly state your main points and provide specific evidence to support your arguments. Avoid making indistinct or general statements that don't provide a direct answer to the question.

For example, based on the previous prompt, a straightforward and direct answer could be: *"In the 18th century, France was ruled by an absolute monarchy, while England was under the governance of a constitutional monarchy. The French economy was primarily agrarian, while the English economy was centered around trade and industry."*

Tip 2: Use Specific Examples and Evidence to Support Your Response

When providing evidence, choose specific examples or details demonstrating your understanding of the topic and directly supporting your main points. Avoid using generalizations or broad statements that do not provide clear evidence.

For instance, in the example prompt, you might discuss how the French monarchy's reliance on the nobility for support led to a heavily agrarian economy, while England's constitutional monarchy encouraged the development of trade and industry through the growth of the merchant class.

Tip 3: Avoid Lengthy Introductions or Conclusions

Given the limited space and word count for SAQs, focus on providing a well-reasoned answer rather than lengthy introductions or conclusions. Instead, spend your time developing clear and concise main points supported by specific evidence.

For instance, rather than initiating with a broad statement like *"The 18th century was a period of significant political and economic change in Europe,"* jump right into the distinctions between the political and economic systems of France and England during that era.

4. Demonstrate Historical Thinking Skills

Despite the limited word count in SAQs, showcasing your historical thinking skills in your responses is essential. Demonstrating your ability to analyze, evaluate, and synthesize historical information will help you earn a higher score on this section of the exam.

Here are some tips for demonstrating historical thinking skills in your SAQ responses:

Tip 1: Show Your Ability to Analyze Cause and Effect, Compare and Contrast, or Identify Continuity and Change

Incorporate analysis of cause and effect, comparison and contrast, or continuity and change in your response to show your understanding of historical processes and relationships. Make connections between events, themes, and concepts to provide a deeper analysis.

When discussing the political and economic systems of 18th-century France and England, explain how these systems influenced social structures, international relations, or cultural developments in each country.

Tip 2: Provide Evidence of Your Understanding of Historical Context, Perspectives, and Significance

Demonstrate your grasp of the historical context by discussing how events, ideas, or trends were affected by or influenced the broader historical landscape. Additionally, consider differing perspectives, like the views of various social groups or countries, to provide a more nuanced analysis.

For example, when comparing and contrasting the political and economic systems of France and England, you might discuss how these systems were shaped by factors like the Enlightenment, religious conflicts, or colonial expansion, and how they influenced the development of other European nations.

Tip 3: Use Relevant Historical Terminology and Concepts Accurately

Employ appropriate historical terminology and concepts in your response to demonstrate your knowledge of the subject matter. Employing accurate terminology can aid you in delivering a clear, logical, and evidence-supported response.

For instance, use phrases **like "absolute monarchy," "constitutional monarchy," "agrarian economy,"** or **"mercantilism"** to portray the political and economic systems of 18th-century France and England.

5. Address All Parts of the Prompt

It's crucial to address all parts of the SAQ prompt in your response. Neglecting to do so may lead to a decreased score, as you may not be completely exhibiting your comprehension of the inquiry or the historical notions it encompasses.

Here are some tips for addressing all parts of the prompt:

Tip 1: Ensure You Answer Each Aspect of the Question Thoroughly

Make sure to address each aspect of the prompt in your response. If the question has multiple parts, answer each part separately and clearly. This will show that you comprehensively understand the topic and can address various components of the question.

Suppose, for instance, that the inquiry requests you to analyze the reasons and repercussions of a significant historical incident. In-depth comprehension of the context helps you evaluate possible answers more accurately, thereby enhancing your chance of picking the correct response.

Tip 2: Clearly Indicate How Your Response Addresses Each Part of the Prompt

As you write your response, make sure to clearly indicate how you are addressing each part of the prompt. Use transitional phrases, topic sentences, or other organizational tools to ensure that your response flows logically and coherently. This will make it simpler for the reader to follow your argument and comprehend how your response addresses the question.

For example, when discussing the causes and effects of a historical event, you might initiate by stating, *"One of the primary catalysts of [event] was...,"* and then later transition to discussing the effects with a phrase such as, *"In the aftermath of [event], several key consequences emerged, including..."*

Tip 3: Check Your Response for Completeness Before Moving On

Before transitioning to the subsequent SAQ, take a moment to review your response and verify that you have covered all parts of the prompt. If you detect any gaps or omissions in your answer, invest the time to refine your response and make it more comprehensive.

6. Manage Your Time Effectively

Time management is critical when answering SAQs on the AP European History exam. With limited time to complete the entire section, it's important to allocate your time wisely to ensure you can answer each question to the best of your ability.

Outlined below are several recommendations for efficiently managing your time when responding to Short Answer Questions (SAQs):

Tip 1: Allocate a Specific Amount of Time for Each SAQ

Ascertain the amount of time you have for the entire SAQ section and divide it by the number of questions to compute how much time you can allocate to each question. In doing so, you can maintain concentration and ensure that you have sufficient time to address each question in the prompt.

For example, if you have 40 minutes for the SAQ section and there are four questions, allocate approximately 10 minutes for each question.

Tip 2: Monitor Your Progress and Adjust Your Pace as Needed

As you progress through the SAQs, keep track of the time and monitor your advancement. If you notice that you're spending an excessive amount of time on a single question, it would be wise to adjust your tempo to ensure that you have sufficient time to address the remaining prompts. Remember, it's more beneficial to provide a comprehensive response to all questions rather than a very detailed answer to just one or two.

Tip 3: Avoid Spending Excessive Time on a Single SAQ

While it's essential to address each SAQ thoroughly, spend only a little bit of time on any single question. All questions are weighted equally, so it's more beneficial to provide a complete and well-reasoned response to each prompt rather than an exceptionally detailed response to one question at the expense of others.

Tip 4: Prioritize Questions You Feel Most Confident About

If you need more time, prioritize answering the questions you feel most confident about to maximize your potential points. This strategy allows you to focus on questions where you have a strong understanding of the historical concepts and can provide a solid response.

Tip 5: Leave Time for Review and Revision

It is recommended that you allocate some time at the conclusion of the SAQ section to review your responses and make any required modifications. This can help you catch errors, omissions, or unclear explanations that may have been overlooked during your initial response.

By incorporating these strategies and maintaining a strong foundation in European history, you can increase your chances of scoring well on the SAQ section, ultimately helping you achieve a high score on the AP European History exam and succeed in your class.

SAMPLE PROMPTS AND MODEL ANSWERS

Below are two sample prompts and model answers for SAQs in the AP European History exam.

Sample Prompt 1:
Explain one major cause of the Protestant Reformation and discuss its significant impact on European society.

Model Answer:

"A principal instigator of the Protestant Reformation was the corruption within the Catholic Church, particularly relating to the sale of indulgences. The sale of indulgences permitted people to secure their entry into heaven by purchasing absolution for their sins. This practice encountered widespread criticism, most notably from Martin Luther, who posited that salvation should be based solely on faith.

A prominent repercussion of the Protestant Reformation on European society was the diminution of the Catholic Church's political influence. As various regions adopted Protestantism, the authority of the Catholic Church and the Pope diminished. This alteration in authority resulted in the emergence of nation-states and the concentration of political influence within monarchies, which were instrumental in molding the political terrain of Europe."

Explanation:

This answer directly addresses both parts of the prompt by explaining a major cause of the Protestant Reformation (corruption within the Catholic Church) and discussing a significant impact on European society (decline of the Catholic Church's political power). The response is concise and specific, providing relevant evidence to support each point.

Sample Prompt 2:

Compare and contrast the social and political effects of the French and Russian revolutions on their respective societies.

Model Answer:

"Both the French and Russian revolutions had profound social and political effects on their respective societies. From a social perspective, both uprisings brought about the deconstruction of the established class systems: the French Revolution eliminated the feudal system and the privileges of the aristocracy, while the Russian Revolution disassembled the social hierarchy and redistributed land to the peasants. Nevertheless, the French Revolution brought about the ascent of the bourgeoisie and the formation of a capitalist society, whereas the Russian Revolution yielded the establishment of a communist state with the ultimate objective of attaining a society free of social classes.

In terms of politics, both revolutions led to the toppling of their corresponding monarchies: the French Revolution culminated in the execution of King Louis XVI and the founding of the First French Republic, while the Russian Revolution led to the abdication of Tsar Nicholas II and the emergence of the Soviet Union. Despite these similarities, the political outcomes of the two revolutions were starkly different. The French Revolution eventually led to the rise of Napoleon Bonaparte and a period of military expansion and dictatorship, while the Russian Revolution brought about the creation of a one-party communist state under the leadership of Vladimir Lenin and, later, Joseph Stalin."

Explanation:

This answer directly addresses the prompt by comparing and contrasting the social and political effects of the French and Russian revolutions. The response is organized and specific, highlighting both similarities (dismantling of class systems and the overthrow of monarchies) and differences (capitalist vs. communist societies and Napoleon vs. Lenin/Stalin) between the two revolutions.

EXCELLING IN THE DBQ (DOCUMENT-BASED QUESTION)

The AP European History exam's Document-Based Question (DBQ) section requires students to analyze and synthesize historical documents to construct a coherent and well-reasoned essay. To excel in this section, developing effective strategies for understanding, analyzing, and integrating the provided documents into a cohesive response is important.

Here are some key steps to master DBQs:

1. Understand the DBQ Prompt

Understanding the prompt will also be an important part of DBQ, just like the other 2 formats of the exam.

2. Analyze the Provided Documents

The next step in mastering DBQs is to carefully analyze the documents provided. These primary and secondary sources will serve as the foundation of your essay, providing evidence and support for your argument.

Here's how to approach the documents:

Step 1: Read Each Document Carefully

Ensure to meticulously read and understand each document. Pay heed to the author, date, context, and any existing bias or perspective. Think about how the source connects to the question and how it can help you prove your point.

Step 2: Annotate the Documents

As you read the documents, annotate them by underlining key points, circling important dates or names, and making notes in the margins. This will help you identify each document's main ideas and supporting evidence, which will be crucial when incorporating them into your essay.

Step 3: Group Documents by Theme or Argument

Once you've analyzed all of the documents, group them by theme or argument. This will help you identify patterns and connections between the documents, making it easier to incorporate them into your essay in a coherent and organized manner.

3. Plan Your Essay

Before you begin writing your DBQ essay, planning your response is essential. This will make sure your essay is well-organized and answers the question well.

Step 1: Develop a Clear Thesis Statement

Your thesis statement should address the prompt and provide a concise argument. It should briefly outline your main points and indicate how you will use the documents to support your argument.

For example, the prompt might read:

"Evaluate the extent to which the Scientific Revolution challenged traditional ideas and institutions in European society."

In this case, a clear thesis statement might be:

"The Scientific Revolution significantly challenged traditional ideas and institutions in European society by promoting empirical observation and skepticism, leading to a reevaluation of long-held beliefs and the eventual decline of the Catholic Church's authority."

Step 2: Outline Your Essay

Create a brief outline of your essay, organizing your main points and supporting evidence. Be sure to incorporate the documents into your outline, noting which documents support each point or argument. The outline should follow a logical structure, with a clear introduction, body paragraphs that address the prompt, and a conclusion that ties everything together.

4. Write Your Essay

With a clear understanding of the prompt, a thorough analysis of the documents, and a well-organized plan, you're ready to write your DBQ essay.

Remember to:
- Start with a strong introduction that includes your thesis statement.
- Use clear topic sentences for each body paragraph that directly relates to your thesis.
- Incorporate the documents into your essay, using them as evidence to support your main points and arguments. Be sure to cite the documents appropriately, either by number or title.
- Analyze and explain the significance of the documents in relation to the prompt, demonstrating your understanding of their content, context, and perspective.
- Provide additional outside information or historical context to further support your argument.
- Use proper historical writing conventions, such as avoiding presentism and using appropriate terminology.
- Finish with a strong ending that backs up your main point and sums up what you've said.

The model answer for the given prompt would be:

" *The Scientific Revolution significantly challenged traditional ideas and institutions in European society by promoting empirical observation and skepticism, leading to a reevaluation of long-held beliefs and the eventual decline of the Catholic Church's authority.*

The Scientific Revolution emphasized the importance of empirical observation and experimentation, directly challenging the traditional reliance on ancient authorities and religious teachings.

For example, Document 1, a passage from Francis Bacon's "Novum Organum," advocates for the use of inductive reasoning and experimentation in the pursuit of knowledge, asserting that "true knowledge can only be derived from direct observation and experimentation." This emphasis on empirical observation undermined the authority of ancient texts and religious doctrine, which had long been European society's primary sources of knowledge.

Similarly, Document 3, an excerpt from Galileo Galilei's "Letter to the Grand Duchess Christina," demonstrates the conflict between scientific inquiry and religious doctrine, as Galileo defends his heliocentric theory against the Catholic Church's geocentric teachings. This clash between scientific discoveries and religious beliefs contributed to a growing skepticism and reevaluation of traditional ideas and institutions.

The Scientific Revolution also led to the decline of the Catholic Church's authority, as demonstrated in Document 2, a political cartoon depicting the trial of Galileo by the Inquisition. The image shows the Catholic Church attempting to suppress scientific inquiry, highlighting the growing tension between religious and secular authorities during this period.

Moreover, the rise of impactful scholars like Isaac Newton, as delineated in Document 4, questioned the Church's command by supporting a systematic perspective of the cosmos. This transformation in perception prepared the path for Enlightenment philosophies, endorsing the disjunction of religious and state institutions and the inception of secular bodies.

In conclusion, the Scientific Revolution significantly challenged traditional ideas and institutions in European society by promoting empirical observation and skepticism. Consequently, long-standing beliefs and religious teachings were scrutinized, and the Catholic Church's authority was undermined. This period of intellectual and cultural metamorphosis formed the bedrock for the Enlightenment and the modern world."

4. Revise and Edit Your Essay

After writing your DBQ essay, revising and editing your work to ensure that it effectively addresses the prompt, incorporates the documents, and presents a clear and well-reasoned argument is essential.

Here are some tips on how to edit and revise your DBQ essay:
Tip 1: Review Your Thesis Statement

Revisit your thesis statement to ensure it addresses the prompt and provides a concise argument. If necessary, make adjustments to your thesis to better reflect the content of your essay and the evidence you've provided.

Tip 2: Check Your Document Integration

Ensure that you have effectively integrated the documents into your essay, using them as evidence to support your main points and arguments. Double-check that you have cited the documents appropriately by number or title and analyzed their significance in relation to the prompt.

Tip 3: Evaluate Your Use of Outside Information

Review your essay to ensure that you have provided additional outside information or historical context to support your argument. Make sure this information is relevant and accurate and that it contributes to your overall argument.

Tip 4: Examine Your Essay Structure

Review your essay for overall organization and coherence. Ensure that your introduction, body paragraphs, and conclusion flow logically and effectively address the prompt. Make any necessary adjustments to improve clarity and readability.

Tip 5: Proofread Your Essay

Finally, conduct a meticulous revision of your paper to rectify any grammar, spelling, or punctuation inaccuracies. Making sure your composition is refined and expertly executed can significantly sway your final score.

By revising and editing your DBQ essay, you can ensure that it effectively addresses the prompt, incorporates the documents, and presents a clear and well-reasoned argument. This attention to detail can help you maximize your score on the DBQ section of the AP European History exam.

SAMPLE PROMPTS AND MODEL ANSWERS

Sample Prompt 1:

Evaluate the extent to which the Congress of Vienna (1814-1815) maintained the balance of power and established lasting peace in Europe.

Model Answer:

"The diplomatic conference known as the Congress of Vienna, which took place from 1814-1815, aimed to reestablish order and peace in Europe following the chaotic period marked by the French Revolution and Napoleonic Wars. Its primary goals were to maintain a power equilibrium among the nations of Europe and cultivate long-term peace across the continent. The Congress largely achieved these objectives, though some underlying tensions and conflicts would eventually reemerge in the 19th and early 20th centuries.

For instance, in document 1, Austrian diplomat Klemens von Metternich, a prominent figure at the Congress of Vienna, underscores the importance of upholding the balance of power in Europe. He contends that it's essential for preserving peace and stability that no single nation dominates the continent. This document demonstrates the Congress of Vienna's primary goal and its participants' diplomatic approach.

Document 2, a British newspaper article from 1815, commends the Congress's efforts to reestablish order and stability in Europe, stating that the agreement has "fostered general tranquility" and "laid the groundwork for enduring peace." This document offers a contemporary view on the perceived success of the Congress of Vienna in accomplishing its objectives.

However, document 3, a political cartoon from 1815, shows European leaders dividing up territory and resources among themselves, with little regard for the people affected by their decisions. This suggests that the Congress of Vienna's focus on maintaining the balance of power may have overlooked the needs and desires of the populations within the territories being redistributed, leading to potential sources of future conflict.

Despite these potential shortcomings, the Congress of Vienna did manage to maintain relative peace and stability in Europe for several decades. Document 4, a letter from Russian Tsar Alexander I to British Foreign Secretary Lord

58

Castlereagh in 1814, accentuates the desire for collaboration and mutual assistance among European powers to ensure peace and prevent future wars.

However, it's crucial to recall that the Congress of Vienna's endeavors to maintain balance of power and secure lasting peace in Europe weren't flawless. The simmering tensions between the escalating forces of nationalism and the conservative ideals of the Congress would ultimately lead to conflicts and revolutions throughout the 19th century, culminating in the World Wars of the 20th century.

In conclusion, the Congress of Vienna significantly accomplished its goals of preserving the balance of power and establishing peace in Europe, as demonstrated by the relative stability and cooperation among European powers in the ensuing decades. However, the Congress's focus on maintaining the old order and disregarding the burgeoning forces of nationalism would eventually contribute to future conflicts and upheavals on the continent."

Explanation:

This model answer effectively addresses the DBQ prompt by evaluating the extent to which the Congress of Vienna maintained the balance of power and established lasting peace in Europe. The response demonstrates a comprehensive understanding of the historical context and the provided documents by using them as evidence to support the argument. The essay begins with a clear thesis statement outlining the main points to be discussed.

The body paragraphs are organized by theme and directly relate to the thesis, using the documents as evidence to support the argument. For example, documents 1 and 2 are used to demonstrate the Congress of Vienna's goals and perceived successes, while document 3 highlights potential flaws in the process. Document 4 is used to emphasize the cooperation and mutual assistance among European powers following the Congress.

Additionally, the essay incorporates outside information, such as the growing forces of nationalism and the conservative ideals of Congress, which provides further context and support for the argument. The concluding section provides an effective summary of the principal arguments and reinforces the thesis, acknowledging the accomplishments of Congress while also acknowledging its constraints.

Sample Prompt 2:

Examine the multiple elements that played a role in the emergence of absolutism in 17th-century France.

Model Answer:

"The 17th century saw France undergo a substantial increase in absolutism, which was marked by the monarchy's unification of authority and control. Multiple factors contributed to this change, including the actions of the Bourbon monarchs, the influence of Cardinal Richelieu followed by Cardinal Mazarin, and the socio-economic conditions of the time.

A central element in the emergence of absolutism in France was the Bourbon rulers, particularly Louis XIII and Louis XIV (document 1). During their rule, the power of the monarchy was substantially broadened as they sought to centralize control and diminish the clout of the nobility. Louis XIV, specifically, is renowned for his famous saying, "L'État, c'est moi" (I am the state), which encapsulates the absolutist ideology perfectly.

Document 2 highlights another vital factor - the sway of Cardinal Richelieu, who acted as the prime advisor to Louis XIII, and later, Cardinal Mazarin, who had a similar role during Louis XIV's rule. Both cardinals enacted policies to fortify the monarchy and centralize authority, such as curbing the Huguenots and reducing noble rights. These endeavors created the groundwork for the expansion of absolutism in France.

Absolutism's emergence in France was also influenced by societal and economic circumstances. The burgeoning wealth of the French monarchy, derived from enhanced taxation and trade, enabled the king to uphold a large standing military and finance ambitious endeavors, like building the Palace of Versailles (document 3). This display of wealth and power further entrenched the authority of the monarchy.

Moreover, the hierarchical organization of French society, with the king at the apex, reinforced the concept of absolute power, as underscored in Document 4. The belief in the divine right of kings, which asserted that rulers were selected by God and accountable only to Him, further justified the French monarchy's power and contributed to the rise of absolutism.

To summarize, the emergence of absolutism in 17th-century France was the result of a confluence of various factors of a political, social, and economic nature. The Bourbon monarchs, the influence of key advisors like Cardinal Richelieu and Cardinal Mazarin, and the social and economic conditions of the time all contributed to the centralization of power and the establishment of an absolute monarchy in France."

Explanation:

This model answer effectively analyzes the various factors that contributed to the rise of absolutism in France during the 17th century. The essay begins with a clear introduction, outlining the main points to be discussed. The body paragraphs are organized by theme, and each paragraph directly relates to the main argument. The provided documents are used as evidence to support the argument, demonstrating a thorough understanding of their content and historical context.

In addition to using the documents, the essay incorporates outside information, such as the role of the Bourbon monarchs and the belief in the divine right of kings, to provide further context and support for the argument. The concluding section offers a concise summary of the primary points and reinforces the overall argument.

TACKLING THE LEQ (LONG ESSAY QUESTION)

The only difference between LEQ from DBQ is that in LEQ, you will not be provided with specific documents to analyze and support your argument. You must instead rely on your knowledge of European history, acquired through your studies and preparation, to compose a coherent and well-organized response.

Strategies for Writing LEQs

1. Read The Prompt Carefully

Carefully read and understand the prompt, just as you would for other essay formats. Identify the key terms, themes, and issues the question addresses.

For example, consider the following prompt:

"Evaluate the extent to which Enlightenment ideas influenced the political development of European nations from 1685 to 1789."

In this prompt, the key terms and themes are **"Enlightenment ideas," "political development,"** and **"European nations."** The time period specified is 1685 to 1789. The question asks you to analyze how Enlightenment ideas influenced political development in European countries during this time.

It is important to understand what the prompt is asking you to do and stay focused on addressing the specific question throughout your essay.

2. Plan Your Response

After understanding the prompt, spend some time brainstorming and organizing your thoughts. Develop a clear thesis statement that directly answers the question and outlines your main points. Create an outline to help structure your essay and ensure a logical flow of ideas.

You can construct a thesis statement by doing the following:

Step 1: Rephrase The Question

You can begin by rephrasing the question in your own words. For example, you could rephrase the prompt as, "To what extent did the ideas of the Enlightenment impact the political development of European nations between 1685 and 1789?"

Step 2: Formulate Your Argument

Next, take a position on the question by formulating your argument. For instance, your argument could be that Enlightenment ideas significantly influenced the political development of European nations during this period.

Step 3: Write Your Thesis Statement

Combine your rephrased question and your argument to create a clear and concise thesis statement.

For the given prompt, a possible thesis statement could be:

"Enlightenment philosophies significantly shaped the political evolution of European nations between 1685 and 1789 by endorsing the principles of logic, personal rights, and power distribution, which contributed to the emergence of constitutional governments and democratic revolutions."

- Next, create an outline to organize your main points and evidence. Remember to:
- Start with a strong introduction that includes your thesis statement.
- Use clear topic sentences for each body paragraph that directly relates to your thesis.
- Include specific examples and evidence to support your argument in each body paragraph.
- Create a conclusion that restates your thesis and summarizes your main points.

3. Use Relevant Historical Evidence

Incorporate specific examples, facts, and events from your studies to support your argument. Ensure that the evidence is relevant to the question and time period. This will demonstrate your knowledge of European history and ability to connect events and developments.

For the given prompt, examples of relevant historical evidence could include:

- Philosophers like John Locke, Voltaire, Montesquieu, and Rousseau, who shaped Enlightenment ideas and influenced political thought.
- The Glorious Revolution in England (1688) established a constitutional monarchy and limited the monarch's power.
- The American Revolution (1775-1783) was influenced by Enlightenment ideas and inspired Europeans to question the authority of their own governments.
- The French Revolution (1789-1799) was driven by the desire for greater political representation, individual rights, and an end to absolutist rule.

4. Analyze and Explain

Don't merely provide a compendium of facts; elucidate the relevance of the evidence you provide and how it substantiates your argument. Assess the origins and effects of historical events and developments, along with their interconnections.

For instance, you might examine how Enlightenment philosophies about power distribution influenced the formation of the United States Constitution, which subsequently inspired political reform movements in Europe. Alternatively, you could scrutinize how the French Revolution epitomized the Enlightenment ideals, such as personal rights and popular sovereignty, while also underlining the challenges and limitations of applying these concepts in reality.

5. Be Mindful of Chronology

Demonstrate your understanding of the historical context by organizing your essay in a chronological manner. This will help you avoid anachronisms and show that you can effectively connect events and developments across time periods.

For instance, you could structure your essay by discussing the influence of Enlightenment ideas on political development in the early, middle, and late stages of the specified time period (1685-1789).

6. Maintain a Clear and Focused Argument

Stay on topic and avoid introducing irrelevant information. Keep your argument focused on the prompt and ensure that each paragraph contributes to your thesis. This will make your essay more coherent and easier to follow.

7. Proofread and Revise

Set aside a portion of your time after the exam to review your essay for potential errors or inconsistencies. Make certain your response is logically organized, connected, and free of spelling and grammatical errors. Check that your argument remains focused on the prompt and that each paragraph contributes to your thesis.

The final answer for the given prompt should look like this:

"Enlightenment philosophies significantly shaped the political evolution of European nations between 1685 and 1789 by endorsing the principles of logic, personal rights, and power distribution, which contributed to the emergence of constitutional governments and democratic revolutions.

The initial stages of this era saw the rise of influential Enlightenment scholars, like John Locke, Voltaire, Montesquieu, and Rousseau, who questioned traditional beliefs and advocated for the importance of reason, individual rights, and the distribution of powers in governance. Their philosophies began to pervade European society, progressively influencing political thought and progression.

In 1688, the Glorious Revolution in England instituted a constitutional monarchy and restricted the monarch's authority, marking a considerable step towards implementing Enlightenment philosophies in governance. This occurrence demonstrated the potential for peaceful political transformation and laid the groundwork for future democratic revolutions.

As the mid-18th century arrived, Enlightenment philosophies' influence continued to broaden, a phenomenon illustrated by the American Revolution (1775-1783). This uprising was propelled by the pursuit for more political representation and individual freedoms, which are fundamental beliefs of Enlightenment thought. The success of the American Revolution motivated Europeans to question their own governments' authority and seek political reform.

Finally, the French Revolution (1789-1799) embodied the Enlightenment ideals, like individual rights and popular sovereignty, while also spotlighting the challenges and constraints of applying these concepts in reality. The revolution signified a turning point in European political evolution, demonstrating the power of the masses to demand change and dismantle the absolutist rule.

Between 1685 and 1789, Enlightenment philosophies had a profound impact on the political progression of European nations. By endorsing the principles of logic, individual rights, and power distribution, these philosophies led to the emergence of constitutional governments and democratic revolutions across the continent. This period of transformation laid the foundation for the modern, democratic Europe we recognize today."

This answer effectively addresses the given prompt, which asked to evaluate the extent to which Enlightenment ideas influenced the political development of European nations from 1685 to 1789. The essay demonstrates a clear understanding of the key themes and time period, and provides a focused and coherent argument supported by relevant historical evidence.

The essay commences with a robust thesis statement that directly responds to the question and sets the scene for the main points discussed in the main paragraphs. The essay body is organized chronologically, facilitating a clear analysis of the influence of Enlightenment philosophies over time. The essay provides specific examples, such as influential Enlightenment philosophers, the Glorious Revolution, the American Revolution, and the French Revolution, to support the argument.

The essay also includes an analysis and explanation of the significance of these events and their connection to Enlightenment ideas. The chronological structure and clear focus on the prompt help maintain a coherent and logical flow throughout the essay.

In the conclusion, the main points are summed up, and the thesis is restated in a way that shows how important the argument is. This essay is an example of a well-crafted response to a long essay question on the AP European History exam, as it adheres to the strategies for writing LEQs and has been proofread and revised.

SAMPLE PROMPTS AND MODEL ANSWER

Sample Prompt 1:

"Analyze the impact of the Scientific Revolution on European society and its relationship with religion between the 16th and 18th centuries."

Model Answer:

"From the 16th to the 18th century, the Scientific Revolution substantially shifted the relationship between European society and religion by challenging conventional beliefs and fostering an emphasis on empirical data, logical thinking, and the application of the scientific process.

Groundbreaking concepts and discoveries by notable figures such as Copernicus, Galileo, Kepler, and Newton during this period disputed the established geocentric view of the cosmos, showcasing the power of empirical evidence and reasoned thought. These scientific advancements contradicted the Catholic Church's teachings, which heavily depended on religious doctrine and the credibility of ancient texts to explain the natural world.

As the Scientific Revolution unfolded, the escalating focus on the scientific method started to undermine the Church's authority, as people increasingly looked for answers through experimentation and empirical observation instead of relying solely on religious teachings. This shift in mentality led to the emergence of secularism, humanism, and skepticism, further diminishing the Church's influence on European society.

Despite these challenges, the Scientific Revolution only partially sever the relationship between European society and religion. Certain scientists, Isaac Newton included, held firm their conviction in a divine entity, attempting to balance their scientific results with their religious beliefs. Additionally, several religious organizations, like the Jesuits, assimilated and utilized the newly acquired scientific knowledge in their teaching systems.

To summarize, the Scientific Revolution greatly impacted the interaction between religion and European society from the 16th to the 18th century. Encouraging empirical analysis and logical reasoning, the Scientific Revolution contested long-held religious beliefs, leading to increased skepticism, secularism, and humanism. However, the relationship between European society and religion was partially severed, as some scientists and religious institutions sought to reconcile the new scientific knowledge with their faith."

Explanation:

This answer effectively addresses the question, which asks the student to analyze the impact of the Scientific Revolution on European society and its relationship with religion between the 16th and 18th centuries. The essay clearly understands the main themes, historical context, and the time period.

The thesis statement unambiguously sets the stage for the essay by establishing its focus, which is the impact of the Scientific Revolution on European society's interaction with religion.

The body of the essay is organized by themes, analyzing how the Scientific Revolution contested the Catholic Church's authority, fostered secularism, skepticism, and humanism, and influenced the relationship between religion and science. The essay also interprets and highlights the importance of these events and their repercussions on European society and religion. Simultaneously, the essay acknowledges that the connection between European society and religion was not entirely severed. Some scientists and religious organizations sought ways to blend their faith with the new scientific knowledge.

The conclusion effectively summarizes the main points of the essay and restates the thesis, emphasizing the profound impact of the Scientific Revolution on European society and its relationship with religion during the specified time period.

Sample Prompt 2:

"Assess the role of women in European society during the Enlightenment and how their status changed as a result of this intellectual movement."

Model Answer:

"The Enlightenment period marked the beginning of changes in women's roles in European society as fresh ideas about individual rights, education, and societal reform challenged traditional gender norms and expectations. Despite being largely excluded from formal education and political power, women significantly influenced intellectual discussions and societal changes during this time.

Women took part in the Enlightenment by participating in salons, social gatherings where intellectuals and philosophers would debate and exchange knowledge. Salons were held by women like Madame de Pompadour, Madame de Stal, and Madame Geoffrin. They brought together the smartest people of their time and gave them a place to talk about ideas and spread Enlightenment ideas.

The Enlightenment also stimulated an increase in support for women's education and rights. Thinkers like Mary Wollstonecraft, the author of "A Vindication of the Rights of Woman," argued that women were equally equipped for logical thought and deserved the same chances for education and self-growth as men. These ideas acted as pillars for the contemporary feminist wave and ignited discussions on the issues of gender parity and women's rights.

While the Enlightenment era signaled some evolutionary shifts for women, it's vital to note that these transformations mainly affected women from the upper-middle and affluent classes. A significant portion of women, particularly those from disadvantaged backgrounds, still encountered considerable socioeconomic barriers hindering their access to educational and self-enhancement opportunities.

In conclusion, the Enlightenment was instrumental in shaping the status of women in European society. The intellectual movement set the stage for future social and political changes by questioning traditional gender roles and fighting for women's rights and education. However, the impact of the Enlightenment on women's status was not uniform, and many women, especially those from lower social classes, continued to face significant barriers to education and opportunities for self-improvement. Overall, the Enlightenment marked an important step toward greater gender equality and the recognition of women's rights, but the full realization of these ideals would require further social and political changes in the centuries that followed."

Explanation:

This answer effectively addresses the question, which asks the student to assess the role of women in European society during the Enlightenment and how their status changed as a result of this intellectual movement. The essay clearly understands the main themes, historical context, and the time period.

The thesis statement clearly establishes the focus of the essay, which is the evolving role of women in European society during the Enlightenment and the changes in their status brought about by the intellectual movement.

The body of the essay is organized thematically, discussing the ways in which women participated in the Enlightenment through salons, the growing support for women's education and rights, and the limitations of these changes for women from lower social classes. The essay also analyzes and explains the significance of these developments and their impact on women's status in European society during the Enlightenment.

The conclusion effectively summarizes the main points of the essay and restates the thesis, emphasizing the crucial role of the Enlightenment in shaping the status of women in European society and the groundwork it laid for future social and political changes. However, the conclusion also acknowledges the limitations of the Enlightenment's impact on women's status and the need for further social and political changes to fully realize gender equality.

COMPREHENSIVE CONTENT REVIEW

Period 1: Renaissance and Reformation (1300-1600)

• Humanism

Humanism was a Renaissance-era intellectual movement that concentrated on the examination of the humanities, encompassing grammar, rhetoric, history, poetry, and moral philosophy. A renewed interest inspired this movement in the classical works of ancient Greece and Rome. Humanist thinkers, including personalities like Petrarch, Erasmus, and Thomas More, assumed that delving into historical works could enhance their understanding of human existence and the world, culminating in a more progressive society.

• Italian Renaissance

The Italian Renaissance, a period of cultural and artistic prosperity extending from the 14th to the 17th century in Italy, primarily in Florence, is characterized by a resurgence of interest in arts, sciences, and humanities. This era saw the birth of artistic methods like perspective, chiaroscuro, and sfumato. The Renaissance era was distinguished by the works of artistic luminaries such as Leonardo da Vinci, Michelangelo, and Raphael.

• Northern Renaissance

The Northern Renaissance was a cultural resurgence in Northern Europe, notably in present-day Germany, the Netherlands, and Belgium, happening concurrently with the Italian Renaissance. Although there was a renewed interest in the arts and humanities, the Northern Renaissance placed a stronger emphasis on religious themes and ordinary life. Jan van Eyck, Albrecht Dürer, and Hieronymus Bosch were key contributors to this movement.

• Protestant Reformation

The Protestant Reformation, starting in the early 16th century, was a reaction to alleged corruption and doctrine discrepancies within the Roman Catholic Church. Often linked to Martin Luther's proclamation of his 95 Theses in 1517, this religious shakeup resulted in the establishment of diverse Protestant factions, encompassing Lutheranism, Calvinism, and Anglicanism.

• Catholic Counter-Reformation

The Counter-Reformation or the Catholic Reformation was the Catholic Church's answer to the Protestant Reformation. The Council of Trent, taking place from 1545 to 1563, served as a foundational element of this reactionary movement. The Church leveraged this forum to define its doctrines, reform its practices, and strive to reclaim those who had converted to Protestantism. Ignatius of Loyola, the founder of the Jesuit order, and Teresa of Ávila were notable figures in this movement.

• Martin Luther

Martin Luther, a German monk and theologian who lived from 1483 to 1546, was a significant catalyst for the Protestant Reformation. He is most well-known for his Ninety-five Theses, which confronted the Church's sale of indulgences and other traditions. Luther underscored the significance of faith, grace, and the supremacy of Scripture over Church tradition in his teachings.

• The Theologian John Calvin

John Calvin (1509-1564) was a French theologian who greatly influenced the establishment of Calvinism, a Protestant faith branch. As discussed in his work "Institutes of the Christian Religion," Calvin's teachings emphasized God's sovereignty, predestination, and the necessity of a disciplined and moral life.

• England's King Henry VIII

Henry VIII (1491-1547), the English monarch, is best known for his numerous marriages and his crucial role in the English Reformation. His move to sever ties with the Catholic Church to divorce Catherine of Aragon and wed Anne Boleyn set the stage for the English Reformation.

• Religious Turmoils

The Reformation period was characterized by religious disputes between Catholics and Protestants, and among various Protestant factions. Wars and political shifts, such as the Schmalkaldic War, the French Wars of Religion, and the Thirty Years' War, occurred due to these disputes. Religious differences and political, territorial, and economic factors drove these wars. The Peace of Westphalia, finalized in 1648, terminated the Thirty Years' War and implemented the principle of cuius regio, eius religio, granting each ruler the authority to dictate the religion of their respective territory.

• Renaissance Art and Culture

Renaissance culture and art were characterized by a resurgence of interest in classical antiquity, humanism, and individualism. Artists, scholars, and writers aimed to emulate and surpass the ancient Greeks and Romans' accomplishments. Renaissance art often portrayed religious subjects, mythological scenes, and daily life. Major advancements in Renaissance art included the development of linear perspective, light and shadow usage, and human anatomy exploration. Leonardo da Vinci, Michelangelo, and Raphael were key artists of the period, while prominent writers included Dante, Petrarch, and Boccaccio.

Period 2: Era of Discovery and Absolute Rule (1450-1750)

• Age of Exploration

The Age of Discovery, extending from the 15th to the 18th centuries, was defined by European exploration and colonization endeavors on a global scale. European explorers and settlers, inspired by a desire for novel trade routes, spreading Christianity, and power amplification, embarked on expeditions to Africa, Asia, and the Americas. During this period, innovations like the astrolabe and magnetic compass revolutionized navigation.

• Columbus

Christopher Columbus (1451-1506), an Italian-born explorer, orchestrated four critical transatlantic voyages. His expeditions, bankrolled by the Spanish Catholic Monarchs, were responsible for introducing Europe to the Americas. Despite indigenous peoples having inhabited these lands for millennia, Columbus's voyages sparked a wave of further exploration and the eventual European colonization of the Americas.

• Magellan

An esteemed Portuguese adventurer, Ferdinand Magellan (~1480-1521), is recognized for initiating the first-ever circumnavigation of the globe. Even though he perished in the Philippines during the journey, his crew successfully completed the round-the-world voyage in 1522, establishing the Earth's roundness and refuting previous assertions that the Americas were part of Asia.

• Vasco da Gama

Vasco da Gama, a Portuguese seafarer (1460-1524), is renowned for being the first European to reach India via the sea. His 1497-1499 journey around Africa's southern tip initiated a direct maritime route to India, bypassing the traditional land routes dominated by Muslim merchants.

• Global Trade Networks

The Age of Exploration stimulated the formation of expansive global trade networks, bridging Europe, Africa, Asia, and the Americas. This interconnection facilitated the exchange of goods, ideas, and populations, leading to technological spread, the rise of formidable trade empires, and the inception of the global economy. Significant trade networks of this period included the triangular Atlantic slave trade, the Indian Ocean trading network, and the Silk Road.

• Mercantilism

Mercantilism, an economic philosophy prevalent in Europe during the Age of Exploration and the early modern era, emphasized wealth accumulation, particularly through gold and silver procurement and a positive trade balance. Mercantilist tactics promoted colonization, the creation of monopolies, and the enhancement of domestic industries.

• Colonization

The Age of Exploration saw European powers establishing colonies across the Americas, Africa, and Asia. These colonial endeavors involved setting up settlements, exploiting resources, and imposing European culture and religion on indigenous communities. The process of colonization led to a significant decrease in indigenous populations in the Americas due to disease, conflict, and forced labor, along with the enforced migration of enslaved Africans via the Atlantic slave trade. The repercussions of European colonization in these regions are still evident in their political, economic, and cultural landscapes.

• Absolutism

Absolutism refers to a form of governance where a single ruler, usually a monarch, wields absolute and unrestricted state control. Under absolutist governance, the monarch is not restrained by laws or other governing bodies and retains the power to dictate all state decisions. Monarchs often validated their rule through the concept of divine right, asserting that their power was granted by God. During this period, potent absolute monarchies surfaced in Europe, including Louis XIV's France, Peter the Great's Russia, and Austria under the Habsburgs.

• Louis XIV

Louis XIV, or the "Sun King," presided over France for a remarkable 72 years, from 1643 to 1715. His reign, marked by centralized governance, military expansion, and patronage of the arts, epitomizes the concept of absolute monarchy. His rule saw the erection of the Palace of Versailles, an emblem of his authority and France's supremacy in Europe.

• Peter the Great

Peter the Great (1672-1725), the Tsar of Russia, held power from 1682 until his death in 1725. His rule was characterized by sweeping reforms aimed at modernizing and Europeanizing Russia. This included the founding of a new capital, Saint Petersburg, and myriad changes in government, military, and societal norms. Peter the Great's reign elevated Russia to become a significant European power, laying the groundwork for Russia's future development and transformation.

• English Civil War

The English Civil War (1642-1651) encompasses a series of conflicts between the Parliamentarians (English Parliament supporters) and the Royalists (supporters of King Charles I). This contention was driven by religious discord, political differences, and power disputes between the monarchy and Parliament. The triumph of the Parliamentarians resulted in Charles I's execution, the brief instatement of a republic under Oliver Cromwell, and ultimately the restoration of the monarchy in 1660.

• Glorious Revolution

The Glorious Revolution of 1688 in England was a non-violent overthrow of King James II by Parliament. This bloodless takeover led to the ascension of Mary II and her husband, William III of Orange, to the throne. Importantly, these Protestant successors replaced James II, a Catholic monarch. This shift signified the onset of the constitutional monarchy in England, as the Bill of Rights andAs a military strategist, he conquered many parts of Europe and created an empire. Following his loss at the Battle of Waterloo in 1815, he was banished to the island of Saint Helena in the Atlantic Ocean, where he met his demise in 1821.

Period 3: Enlightenment and Revolution (1600-1800)

• Enlightenment

Spanning the 17th to 18th centuries, the Enlightenment or the Age of Reason, was an influential movement that celebrated reason, individualism, and skepticism. The intellectual landscape was transformed as traditional ideas were challenged, and a culture of rational inquiry was promoted. Leading minds such as John Locke, Montesquieu, Rousseau, and Voltaire were instrumental in applying scientific methods to the investigation of society, paving the way for advancements in philosophy, politics, and the physical sciences.

• Scientific Revolution

The Scientific Revolution, a transformative period from the 16th to the 18th centuries, brought profound developments in the natural sciences, mathematics, and astronomy. The scientific method emerged during this era, underscoring empirical observation, experimentation, and rational interpretation. Important personalities of the Scientific Revolution included Nicolaus Copernicus, Galileo Galilei, Johannes Kepler, and Isaac Newton.

• John Locke

An eminent Enlightenment philosopher, John Locke (1632-1704), was an English thinker specializing in politics and philosophy. Locke's works, namely "Two Treatises of Government" and "An Essay Concerning Human Understanding," deeply shaped the era, propagating crucial notions such as natural rights, the social contract, and the legitimate overthrow of a despotic government that doesn't uphold its citizens' rights.

• Montesquieu

Montesquieu (1689-1755), a French philosopher and theorist, advocated for the principle of power segregation within a government. In his landmark work "The Spirit of the Laws," he proposed that preserving individual liberties and averting tyranny could be achieved by dispersing political power across various governmental branches. This concept profoundly influenced the authors of the United States Constitution.

• Rousseau

Jean-Jacques Rousseau (1712-1778), a French philosopher and author, produced influential texts like "The Social Contract" and "Émile," which explored the relationship between personal freedom and social duty. He posited that society should be governed by the collective will of its citizens, and individuals should willingly subject themselves to this collective will to preserve their liberty.

• Voltaire

Voltaire (1694-1778), a distinguished French writer and philosopher, was a passionate advocate for freedom of expression and religious tolerance. His writings, such as "Candide" and "Letters on England," condemned the abuse of power by the Church and the state, ardently endorsing Enlightenment ideals of rationality, tolerance, and progress.

• French Revolution

The French Revolution, unfolding from 1789 to 1799, marked a period of significant social and political tumult in France. It resulted in the fall of the Bourbon monarchy, the emergence of radical political groups, and eventually led to Napoleon Bonaparte's rise to power. Spurred by Enlightenment ideas, economic struggles, and aspirations for democratic change and societal equality, the Revolution brought enduring transformation to French society.

• American Revolution

The American Revolution transpired from 1765 to 1783, culminating in a war between Great Britain and its thirteen North American colonies, which declared their independence as the United States of America. Triggered by conflicts over taxation, representation, and Britain's heightened control, the Revolution ended with the Treaty of Paris in 1783, which recognized the United States' independence and defined its borders.

• Haitian Revolution

The Haitian Revolution (1791-1804) was a victorious uprising against colonial authority and slavery in the French colony of Saint-Domingue, leading to the creation of Haiti as an independent nation. Influenced by Enlightenment and French Revolution ideologies, the Haitian Revolution deeply disrupted the racial and societal structures of its epoch.

• Napoleon Bonaparte

Napoleon Bonaparte, a key figure in French military and government from 1769 to 1821, gained prominence during the French Revolution and subsequent wars. As the Emperor of France, Napoleon built a vast empire dominating large swathes of Europe and introduced a series of administrative and legal reforms known as the Napoleonic Code. He was instrumental in the establishment of several Latin American countries as independent states, earning the nickname "The Liberator."

• Congress of Vienna

The Congress of Vienna (1814-1815) was a conference of European powers convened to redraw the political boundaries of Europe following the fall of Napoleon. The main goals of the Congress were to restore the balance of power in Europe, restore the Bourbon monarchy in France, and contain the spread of revolutionary ideas. The Congress established a conservative international order known as the Concert of Europe to maintain stability and prevent future wars.

Period 4: Industrialization and Nationalism (1750-1900)

• Industrial Revolution

During the Industrial Revolution, the economy, cities, and factories all experienced rapid growth. It started in Britain at the end of the 18th century and spread to other countries in Europe and the US in the 19th century. The Industrial Revolution was marked by new technologies like steam engines, railroads, and mechanized textile production. It was also marked by the growth of factories and the increase in the number of people who worked.

• Urbanization

People migrate from the country to the city in search of employment and a better quality of life. This is called "urbanization." During the Industrial Revolution, urbanization accelerated as factories and other industries were built in and around cities, drawing workers from the countryside. This rapid urbanization led to overcrowding, poor living conditions, and various social and environmental problems.

• Capitalism

The pursuit of profit and private ownership of the means of production are the foundations of capitalism as an economic system. Modern capitalism, which is characterized by extensive industrial production, wage labor, and competitive markets, was developed as a result of the Industrial Revolution. Capitalism contributed to the growth of the global economy, as well as to significant social and economic inequality.

• Labor Movements

As a response to the harsh working conditions and low wages faced by many workers during the Industrial Revolution, labor movements emerged to advocate for better working conditions, higher wages, and other workers' rights. These movements often took the form of trade unions, which sought to collectively bargain with employers and sometimes engaged in strikes and other forms of protest.

• Karl Marx

Karl Marx (1818-1883) was a German philosopher, economist, and political theorist who co-authored "The Communist Manifesto" with Friedrich Engels and wrote "Das Kapital." Marx's theories critiqued the capitalist system and its inherent inequalities, arguing that history was shaped by class struggle and that capitalism would eventually be replaced by a socialist and communist society, where the means of production would be owned and controlled by the working class.

• Nationalism

Nationalism is a political ideology that emphasizes a group of people's shared culture, history, and identity and advocates for their self-determination and political sovereignty. During the 19th century, nationalism fueled the unification of Italy and Germany and various independence movements in Europe and the Americas.

• Italian Unification

Italian Unification, also known as the Risorgimento, was the political and social movement that consolidated the various states on the Italian Peninsula into the Kingdom of Italy in the mid-19th century. Key figures in the unification process included Giuseppe Mazzini, Camillo di Cavour, and Giuseppe Garibaldi.

• German Unification

German Unification was the process by which the various German states were unified into a single nation-state, the German Empire, under the leadership of Prussian Chancellor Otto von Bismarck in 1871. Bismarck used both military force and diplomacy to bring Germany together. His "blood and iron policy" led to the Franco-Prussian War and the creation of the German Empire, which was announced in the Hall of Mirrors at the Palace of Versailles.

• Imperialism

The practice of expanding a nation's power and influence through colonization, military force, or other means is known as imperialism. European nations raced to establish colonies and spheres of influence around the world in the late 19th and early 20th centuries, especially in Africa and Asia. Economic, political, and cultural factors, including the desire for new markets and resources, national prestige, and a belief in the superiority of European civilization, drove this era of imperialism.

• Scramble for Africa

The Scramble for Africa was the competition between European powers to colonize and control territories in Africa during the late 19th and early 20th centuries. This process was characterized by a rapid partitioning of the African continent, with European powers establishing colonies and protectorates that encompassed nearly the entire continent by 1914. The Scramble for Africa had significant political, economic, and social consequences for both Africa and Europe, including exploiting African resources, suppressing African political and cultural autonomy, and intensifying European rivalries.

Period 5: 19th Century and Early 20th Century European Society and Culture (1815-1914)

• Romanticism

Romanticism was an artistic, literary, and intellectual movement that originated in Europe in the late 18th century and continued through the mid-19th century. As a reaction to the rationalism of the Enlightenment and the social and political changes brought about by the Industrial Revolution, Romanticism emphasized emotion, imagination, and individualism. Poets like William Wordsworth, Samuel Taylor Coleridge, and Lord Byron, as well as artists like Caspar David Friedrich and J.M.W. Turner, were prominent members of the Romantic movement.

• Realism

Realism was an artistic and literary movement that emerged in the mid-19th century as a response to Romanticism. Realist artists and writers sought to depict everyday life and ordinary people as they truly were, often focusing on the harsh realities of industrial society and the struggles of the working class. Notable realist authors included Gustave Flaubert, Emile Zola, and Charles Dickens, while realist painters included Gustave Courbet and Jean-François Millet.

• Social Reform Movements

In the 19th and early 20th centuries, various social reform movements emerged in response to the social and economic challenges posed by the Industrial Revolution and urbanization. These movements sought to improve living and working conditions, promote education, and address social problems such as poverty, crime, and alcoholism. Key reform movements of this period included the temperance movement, the public health movement, and the movement for educational reform.

• Women's Suffrage

The women's suffrage movement sought to secure the right to vote for women and promote gender equality in society. The movement gained momentum throughout the 19th and early 20th centuries, leading to the gradual extension of voting rights to women in many countries, including the United Kingdom in 1918 and the United States in 1920.

• Nationalism

As previously mentioned, nationalism significantly shaped European society and politics during the 19th century. In addition to driving the unification of Italy and Germany, nationalism contributed to the rise of independence movements in the Balkans and the emergence of ethnic tensions within multiethnic empires such as the Austro-Hungarian Empire and the Ottoman Empire.

• Imperialism

As we've already talked about, imperialism was the most important thing in the late 19th and early 20th centuries, when European powers were trying to grow their empires and take control of places outside of Europe. This era of imperialism had profound consequences for global politics and economics, as well as for the cultures and societies of both colonized and colonizing nations.

• Technological Advancements

The 19th and early 20th centuries saw a range of important technological advancements that transformed European society and the global economy. The steam engine, the telegraph, the telephone, and the internal combustion engine changed transportation, communication, and manufacturing. New scientific discoveries and theories, like Darwin's theory of evolution and the germ theory of disease, changed how we think about the world.

• Belle Epoque

The Belle Epoque (1871-1914) was a period of relative peace, prosperity, and cultural innovation in Europe, particularly in France. This era saw the rise of new artistic movements, such as Art Nouveau and the avant-garde, as well as advancements in science, technology, and urban planning. The Belle Epoque ended abruptly with the outbreak of World War I in 1914.

• World War I

World War I (1914-1918) was a global conflict that involved many of the world's major powers, including the Allies (led by France, Russia, and the United Kingdom) and the Central Powers (led by Germany, Austria-Hungary, and the Ottoman Empire). Trench warfare, new military technologies, and unprecedented levels of destruction and casualties characterized the war. World War I reshaped the political landscape of Europe and set the stage for further conflicts and tensions in the 20th century.

• Cultural Changes

The 19th and early 20th centuries saw significant cultural changes in Europe as industrialization, urbanization, and new ideas about politics, art, and science transformed traditional societies and ways of life. These changes were reflected in the emergence of new artistic and literary movements, the growth of mass culture and consumerism, and the development of new social organization and activism forms.

Period 6: Interwar Years and World War II (1919-1945)

• Treaty of Versailles

The Allies and Germany signed the Treaty of Versailles in 1919 to officially end the First World War. The treaty imposed severe financial reparations and territorial losses on Germany and the disarmament of its military. The harsh terms of the treaty, particularly the "war guilt" clause that placed sole blame for the war on Germany, contributed to political and economic instability in Germany and fueled resentment that would later lead to World War II.

• Russian Revolution

The Russian Revolution of 1917 led to the overthrow of the Russian monarchy, the rise of the Bolshevik Party, and the formation of the Soviet Union. Widespread discontent with the autocratic rule of Tsar Nicholas II, the economic hardships of World War I, and the influence of Marxist ideas drove the revolution.

• Rise of Fascism

Fascism is a far-right, authoritarian political ideology that emerged in the interwar period, characterized by dictatorial power, forcible suppression of opposition, and a focus on nationalism and often racism. The rise of fascism in Europe was driven by economic and political instability following World War I and by disillusionment with liberal democracy and the spread of communist ideas. Key fascist regimes included those of Benito Mussolini in Italy and Adolf Hitler in Germany.

• Great Depression

The Great Depression, which happened from 1929 to 1939, was a big drop in the economy around the world. It started in the United States and spread to Europe and other places. The depression was characterized by high unemployment, widespread poverty, and a sharp decline in industrial production and international trade. The Great Depression had significant social, political, and economic consequences, including the rise of extremist political movements and the implementation of new economic policies and social welfare programs in many countries.

• Spanish Civil War

The Spanish Civil War happened from 1936 to 1939. It was a fight between the right-wing Nationalist rebels led by General Francisco Franco and the Republican government of Spain. The war was marked by atrocities committed by both sides and served as a testing ground for the military tactics and weapons that would be used in World War II. The Nationalists eventually emerged victorious, establishing a fascist dictatorship under Franco that would last until his death in 1975.

• World War II

World War II (1939-1945) was a global conflict that involved the majority of the world's nations, including the major powers of the Allies (led by the United States, the Soviet Union, and the United Kingdom) and the Axis (led by Germany, Italy, and Japan). The war was characterized by large-scale military campaigns, the Holocaust, and the use of nuclear weapons. World War II resulted in tens of millions of deaths, redrawing of national borders, and the emergence of the United States and the Soviet Union as superpowers.

• Holocaust

The Holocaust was the systematic genocide of approximately six million European Jews and millions of other targeted groups by Nazi Germany and its collaborators during World War II. The Holocaust was carried out through mass shootings, forced labor, and extermination camps, representing one of the darkest and most tragic chapters in human history.

Period 7: Post-World War II Europe and the Cold War (1945-1991)

• Cold War

During the Cold War, which lasted from 1947 to 1991, the US and its allies (called the Western Bloc) and the USSR and its allies (called the Eastern Bloc) were at odds on the world stage. The conflict was characterized by ideological differences, military buildups, espionage, and proxy wars, but it never escalated into a full-scale war between the two superpowers. In 1991, the dissolution of the Soviet Union marked the end of the Cold War.

• Marshall Plan

The Marshall Plan (1948-1952) was a U.S. economic aid program designed to help rebuild Western European economies after the devastation of World War II. The plan provided billions of dollars in financial assistance and technical expertise, and it played a major role in Europe's postwar recovery and economic growth.

• European Integration

In the aftermath of World War II, European nations began a process of economic and political integration to foster cooperation and prevent future conflicts. This process led to the establishment of institutions such as the European Coal and Steel Community (1951), the European Economic Community (1957), and the European Union (1993).

• Decolonization

Decolonization refers to the process by which European colonial powers granted independence to their colonies, primarily in Africa and Asia, in the decades following World War II. Various factors, including nationalist movements in the colonies, the weakening of European powers after the war, and international pressure for self-determination and human rights, drove decolonization.

• Fall of Communism and the Soviet Union

Between the end of the 1980s and the beginning of the 1990s, communism in Eastern Europe and the Soviet Union fell apart. This was a long process. Factors contributing to the collapse of communism included economic stagnation, political corruption, the growing influence of Western culture and ideas, and the policies of Soviet leader Mikhail Gorbachev, such as glasnost (openness) and perestroika (restructuring). In 1989, the fall of the Berlin Wall signified the end of the Cold War and the beginning of Germany's reunification. The Soviet Union officially dissolved in 1991, leading to the emergence of 15 independent republics, including Russia.

Period 8: Contemporary Europe (1991-Present)

• European Union

The European Union (EU) was established in 1993 as a political and economic union of European countries. The European Union has created a single market that allows for the free movement of goods, services, capital, and people, as well as a common currency, the euro. The EU has played a significant role in shaping modern European politics, economics, and culture, and it has expanded its membership to include many former communist countries from Eastern Europe.

• Balkan Wars and Ethnic Conflicts

The Balkan Wars of the 1990s were a series of violent conflicts in the former Yugoslavia, which broke apart along ethnic lines following the collapse of communism. These conflicts, which included the Bosnian War and the Kosovo War, were marked by brutal ethnic cleansing, war crimes, and large-scale displacement of civilians. International interventions, peace agreements, and the establishment of war crimes tribunals have sought to bring stability and justice to the region.

• Globalization

Globalization is the process of increasing economic, political, and cultural interconnectedness among nations around the world. In contemporary Europe, globalization has led to increased trade and investment, the spread of technology and information, and the growth of multinational corporations. Globalization has also raised concerns about the loss of national sovereignty, cultural homogenization, and the potential for economic and social inequality.

• Migration and Multiculturalism

In recent decades, Europe has experienced significant migration from outside the continent, particularly from Africa, the Middle East, and Asia. This influx of migrants and refugees has increased cultural diversity and raised complex issues related to integration, multiculturalism, and social cohesion. Debates over immigration and national identity have become prominent in European politics and society.

• Rise of Populism and Euroscepticism

The rise of populism and Euroscepticism in Europe has been driven by factors such as economic inequality, concerns about immigration, and disillusionment with the European Union and traditional political parties. Populist movements and political parties have gained support in many European countries, leading to shifts in the political landscape and raising questions about the future of European integration and liberal democracy.

• Climate Change and Environmental Challenges

Like the rest of the world, Europe faces significant challenges related to climate change and environmental degradation. European countries have been at the forefront of efforts to combat climate change by developing renewable energy, implementing carbon pricing, and participating in international climate agreements. However, the scale of the challenge necessitates ongoing commitment and innovation in order to mitigate the worst effects of climate change and ensure a sustainable future.

• Terrorism

In recent years, Europe has experienced a number of high-profile terrorist attacks perpetrated primarily by individuals or groups inspired by extremist ideologies. These attacks have targeted major cities, public spaces, and cultural events, and they have heightened concerns about security and social cohesion. European governments have responded with a range of counterterrorism measures, including increased surveillance, intelligence sharing, and efforts to counter radicalization.

• Digital Revolution and the Information Age

The digital revolution and the rise of the information age have profoundly transformed European society, the economy, and culture. The widespread adoption of the internet, smartphones, and other digital technologies has facilitated new forms of communication, commerce, and creative expression, while also raising concerns about privacy, disinformation, and the impact of technology on mental health and well-being.

• Brexit

Brexit refers to the United Kingdom's decision to leave the European Union following a 2016 referendum in which a majority of UK voters chose to leave the bloc. The Brexit process was marked by complex negotiations, political divisions, and economic uncertainty, and it raised important questions about the future of the European Union, the UK's relationship with Europe, and the broader forces shaping global politics.

• Ongoing Conflicts and Crises

Contemporary Europe continues to face a range of conflicts and crises, both within its borders and in its relations with other countries and regions. Ongoing issues include territorial disputes, such as the conflict between Russia and Ukraine, political instability in countries like Belarus, and humanitarian crises related to migration and refugees. Addressing these challenges will require cooperation, diplomacy, and innovative peace-building and conflict-resolution approaches.

• European Response to the COVID-19 Pandemic

The COVID-19 pandemic has profoundly impacted Europe and the world, leading to widespread illness, death, and disruption of daily life. European countries have responded to the pandemic in various ways, including implementing lockdowns, promoting social distancing, and distributing vaccines. The pandemic has also brought attention to the value of international cooperation in resolving international health emergencies and has caused a renewed emphasis on bolstering healthcare infrastructure and pandemic preparedness.

• The Rise of China and the Changing Global Order

As China's economic and political influence has grown, Europe has been faced with new challenges and opportunities in its relations with the rising superpower. European countries have engaged in trade, investment, and diplomatic initiatives with China while expressing concerns about human rights, intellectual property, and security. The rise of China has contributed to a shifting global order, and Europe will need to navigate this new landscape while maintaining its core values and interests.

• The Future of the European Union

The European Union faces a number of pressing challenges and questions about its future direction, including issues related to further integration, enlargement, democratic legitimacy, and the balance of power between member states and EU institutions. European leaders and citizens will need to engage in a robust debate about the future of the EU and its role in a rapidly changing world.

• Demographic Changes and the Aging Population

Europe is experiencing significant demographic changes, with low birth rates and longer life expectancies leading to an aging population. This trend has implications for social welfare systems, healthcare, the labor market, and intergenerational relations. European countries will need to develop innovative policies and strategies to address the challenges posed by demographic change and ensure all citizens' well-being.

• Education and the Future of Work

The changing nature of work, driven by technological advancements and globalization, has led to new opportunities and challenges for European societies. As old industries go away and new ones start up, education and workforce development policies are needed more and more to give people the skills and knowledge they need to do well in the 21st-century economy. European countries must invest in education, training, and lifelong learning in order to promote social mobility, economic growth, and social cohesion.

EXAM PREPARATION

Exam preparation is crucial for success on the AP European History exam.

Follow these strategies and tips to make sure you're ready and confident on test day:

1. Create a Study Plan

Creating a study plan is essential in preparing for the AP European History exam. An efficiently structured study regimen can ensure you stay focused, use your time optimally, and cover all necessary material before your examination.

Here are a few recommendations for constructing a practical study timetable:

a. Set Clear Goals

Begin by setting specific, measurable, and attainable goals for your exam preparation. These goals could include desired scores on practice exams, completion of specific chapters or themes, or mastering certain historical thinking skills.

You could aim to achieve an average score of 80% in multiple-choice practice questions, complete a comprehensive overview of the Enlightenment era, or become proficient at comparing and contrasting historical events. This will help keep your focus on what needs to be accomplished and monitor your progression as you study.

b. Break Down the Course Content

Partition the syllabus into digestible portions, such as chronologically ordered periods, themes, or significant occurrences.

Possessing a structured system for studying could be advantageous in ensuring that all relevant topics are reviewed in a systematic manner. This approach can aid in effectively managing time and preparing for exams or other academic tasks.

You could categorize your study plan into sections like the Renaissance and Reformation, the Age of Exploration, the Enlightenment, the French Revolution and Napoleon, the Industrial Revolution, the World Wars, and the Cold War and European integration, for example.

c. Allocate Time and Resources

Ascertain your available time before the test and distribute it adequately among each section of your study plan. Consider factors like the difficulty of the material, your existing knowledge about the topics, and the relevance of each section in the context of the test.

Also, specify the resources you will utilize for each section, like textbooks, study guides, online resources, or study groups.

Create a detailed schedule outlining the specific tasks and activities you will complete for each study plan section. Be pragmatic about the amount of time you can allocate to studying each day or week and ensure you have sufficient time to review and rehearse the necessary material.

For instance, allocate two weeks to study the Renaissance and Reformation using a mix of your textbook, online resources, and a study group.

Your schedule could include the following:
- Reading and taking notes on specific chapters.
- Reviewing key concepts and events.
- Practicing essay questions.
- Participating in group discussions.

d. Monitor Your Progress

Regularly assess your progress towards your goals and adjust your study plan as needed. This could involve revisiting certain subjects, allocating more time to specific sections, or incorporating additional resources. Tracking your progress will aid in maintaining focus and motivation while also identifying areas that may need further focus or improvement.

For instance, if you require assistance with multiple-choice questions about the Industrial Revolution. In that case, adjust your study plan to allocate more time to review that period, practice additional questions, or seek help from a study group or tutor.

e. Plan for Review and Practice

Include time in your study plan to review previously studied material and practice various question types. Regular review and practice will help reinforce your knowledge and improve your test-taking skills.

Schedule periodic review sessions to go over key concepts, events, and themes from earlier sections of your study plan. Additionally, allocate time for practicing multiple-choice, short-answer, document-based, and long essay questions to become more comfortable with each question format and improve your overall exam performance.

f. Stay Flexible and Adapt

Be aware that your study plan may need adjustments as you progress in your preparation. Stay flexible and modify your plan as necessary to address any obstacles, changes in your schedule, or new information that arises. A successful study plan is one that evolves to meet your needs and ensures that you are well-prepared for the AP European History exam.

By creating a comprehensive and flexible study plan, you will be better prepared to confidently tackle the AP European History exam, achieve your desired scores, and increase your chances of scoring a 5 on exam day.

2. Develop Time Management Skills

Developing time management skills is essential for success in the AP European History exam. Efficient time management will enable you to complete each section of the test within the designated time, ensuring you can answer all questions without rushing your responses.

Here are some strategies for enhancing your time management skills:

a. Understand the Exam Structure

Get acquainted with the format and timing of the test. Understanding how much time you have for each section (multiple-choice, short-answer, document-based, and long essay questions) will help you pace yourself and distribute your time effectively during the test.

b. Practice Under Timed Conditions

Simulate exam conditions by practicing with sample questions under timed constraints. This will help you adjust to the time constraints and gain a better understanding of how long each question type requires.

c. Develop a Test-Taking Strategy

Formulate a plan for tackling each section of the test, including the sequence in which you will answer the questions and the amount of time you will allocate to each. For instance, you could begin with the multiple-choice questions, then proceed to the short-answer questions, and finally attempt the document-based and long essay questions. Be prepared to modify your approach if required during the test.

d. Prioritize Questions

Learn to prioritize questions based on their difficulty and point value. Prioritize answering the questions you are most confident about before moving on to the more difficult ones. This will help you maximize your score and ensure you secure all available points.

e. Pace Yourself

Monitor your time while testing and adjust your pace as needed. Be conscious of the time spent per question and avoid dedicating an excessive duration to a single query. If you find yourself unable to move forward with a question, make an educated guess and move on.

f. Practice Active Reading

Boost your reading speed and comprehension by practicing active reading strategies, such as skimming, annotating, and summarizing. This will enable you to assimilate information more quickly and effectively, which is particularly important for document-based and long essay questions.

Effective time management ensures you assign appropriate time to each section of the exam, enabling you to answer all questions and generate well-considered responses.

3. Stay Informed on Current Events

Staying informed on current events benefits your general knowledge and can enhance your understanding of historical events and themes in the AP European History course. By keeping abreast with world affairs, you can establish connections between historical and current events, cultivate a comprehensive view of international matters, and hone your analytical and critical reasoning skills.

Here are a few suggestions to keep you updated with ongoing events:
a. Read News from Reputable Sources
Regularly read news articles from trustworthy sources such as The New York Times, The Guardian, The Economist, or BBC News. Make sure to choose a variety of sources to get different perspectives on the events unfolding in Europe and around the world.

b. Follow International News Outlets
Broaden your worldview by following international news outlets, offering additional viewpoints and perspectives on European and worldwide events. Some examples include Le Monde, Der Spiegel, and El País.

c. Utilize News Aggregators
Use news aggregators like Google News, Apple News, or Feedly to compile news articles from multiple sources, allowing you to stay informed on a wide range of topics and perspectives.

d. Engage in Social Media Wisely
Follow reputable news organizations, journalists, or experts on social media platforms like Twitter or Facebook for updates and analysis of current events. Be cautious of misinformation and verify information from reliable sources before accepting it as fact.

e. Participate in Discussions and Debates
Join online forums or discussion groups, or participate in in-person debates, to discuss current events with peers, teachers, or experts. This will help you develop your critical thinking and analytical skills and expand your understanding of different viewpoints.

f. Relate Current Events to Course Content
As you stay informed on current events, make connections to the historical events and themes covered in your AP European History course. This will help you contextualize historical events and better understand the course material.

g. Schedule Regular News Updates

Set aside time in your daily or weekly routine to catch up on current events. Consistency is key when staying informed; scheduling regular news updates can help you make it a habit.

By staying informed on current events, you will enrich your understanding of European history, develop valuable skills, and make connections between the past and present, ultimately enhancing your performance on the AP European History exam.

4. Take Care of Yourself

Taking care of yourself is essential for achieving success on the AP European History exam and maintaining overall well-being. A healthy body and mind contribute to better focus, memory retention, and stress management.

Here are some suggestions for self-care during the exam preparation period:

a. Get Enough Sleep

Ample sleep is vital for brain function, memory consolidation, and emotional stability. Try to ensure 7-9 hours of rest each night to keep your body and mind rejuvenated and ready for studying and exams.

b. Eat a Balanced Diet

A nutrient-rich, balanced diet can supply the energy and mental clarity necessary for effective study and exam performance. Incorporate fruits, vegetables, whole grains, lean proteins, and healthy fats into your daily meals and snacks.

c. Stay Hydrated

Staying properly hydrated is vital for overall brain and body health. Drink water consistently throughout the day and avoid excessive caffeine or sugary beverages that can lead to dehydration and energy slumps.

d. Exercise Regularly

Regular exercise can alleviate stress, lift your spirits, and improve mental sharpness. Strive to engage in at least 30 minutes of moderate-intensity physical activity on most days of the week, which could include activities such as fast-paced walking, swimming, cycling, or any other activity you enjoy.

e. Manage Stress
Discover healthy strategies to handle stress and anxiety while preparing for an examination. Techniques like deep breathing, sequential muscle relaxation, meditation, or yoga can help maintain calm and focus.

f. Take Breaks
Plan breaks into your study sessions to avoid getting too tired and to keep working well. Use the Pomodoro Technique (25 minutes of focused work followed by a 5-minute break) or another time management method that works for you.

g. Maintain a Social Life
Maintain contact with family and friends while studying for an exam to maintain a support system and reduce stress. Engage in enjoyable activities like watching a movie or going out for dinner to maintain a healthy balance between studying and relaxation.

h. Seek Help When Needed
If you're struggling with exam preparation, stress, or personal issues, don't hesitate to seek help from teachers, counselors, family members, or friends. They can provide guidance, support, and resources to help you navigate challenges and succeed in your AP European History exam preparation.

Taking care of yourself during the exam preparation period will create a strong foundation for effective studying and peak performance on the AP European History exam. Remember that your well-being is equally as important as academic achievement.

CONCLUSION

Embarking on a journey through European history and ultimately completing the AP European History exam offers a distinct chance to broaden one's knowledge and foster critical thinking, analytical aptitude, and a heightened sense of admiration for the forces that have influenced our contemporary world. These proficiencies not only prove advantageous in academic pursuits but also provide lifelong advantages that transcend the boundaries of the classroom. By embracing this challenge, you immerse yourself n a realm of discovery and personal growth, broadening your horizons and contributing to your intellectual development.

As you start this adventure, it's critical to ready yourself in detail, cultivate effective learning practices, and refine your examination techniques to optimize your potential for achieving stellar results in the AP European History test. Keep in mind, your steadfast commitment and diligent efforts will be rewarded as you aim for a top score of 5 on the exam, outperform in your class, and garner an enriched comprehension of European chronicles.

Maintaining a healthy equilibrium between studying and self-care is equally essential. Ensuring physical, emotional, and mental well-being is vital, as these elements significantly contribute to your overall health and academic success.

By following the strategies and tips outlined in this study guide, you will be well-equipped to navigate the AP European History course and exam challenges. Remain attentive, determined, and believe in your competencies, seizing this chance to enhance your knowledge, mature, and excel in your scholarly pursuits.

Good luck on your AP European History journey, and may it be a rewarding and fulfilling experience that paves the way for continued success in your future academic and professional pursuits.

RESOURCES AND TOOLS

• "Western Civilization: A Brief History" by Jackson J. Spielvogel (https://www.amazon.com/Western-Civilization-Brief-History-Volume/dp/1305091469)

• "Cracking the AP European History Exam" by The Princeton Review (https://www.amazon.com/Princeton-Review-European-History-Premium/dp/0593450795/ref=sr_1_2?crid=1ZWYFZP6P2ALA&keywords=Cracking+the+AP+European+History+Exam+2022&qid=1681542603&s=books&sprefix=cracking+the+ap+european+history+exam+2022%2Cstripbooks-intl-ship%2C315&sr=1-2)

• "AP European History Premium" by Seth A. Roberts M.A (https://www.amazon.com/European-History-Premium-2022-2023-Comprehensive/dp/1506278485/ref=sr_1_2?crid=33E60W4B74TBI&keywords=AP+European+History+Exam&qid=1681542697&s=books&sprefix=ap+european+history+exa%2Cstripbooks-intl-ship%2C331&sr=1-2)

• "Western Civilization: Ideas, Politics, and Society" by Marvin Perry et al. (https://www.amazon.com/Western-Civilization-Ideas-Politics-Society/dp/1305091396)

• Khan Academy: AP European History (https://www.khanacademy.org/humanities/renaissance-reformation)

• AP Classroom: AP European History (https://apcentral.collegeboard.org/courses/ap-european-history/classroom-resources)

• Quizlet - AP European History (https://quizlet.com/subject/ap-european-history/)

• Crash Course European History on YouTube
(https://www.youtube.com/playlist?list=PL8dPuuaLjXtNjasccl-
WajpONGX3zoY4M)

• Tom Richey's AP European History channel on YouTube
(https://www.youtube.com/user/tomforamerica/playlists)

Made in the USA
Las Vegas, NV
02 October 2024

96103701R00063